I SWEAR
I WAS THERE

DAVID NOLAN is an award-winning author, journalist and television producer. He's written and produced documentaries on the Sex Pistols, The Smiths, Echo and the Bunnymen and the free festival movement of the Seventies. He's also written books about Bernard Sumner, Damon Albarn, Tony Wilson, Ed Sheeran and even Simon Cowell.

I SWEAR I WAS THERE

SEX PISTOLS, MANCHESTER AND THE GIG THAT CHANGED THE WORLD

DAVID NOLAN

MUSIC
PRESS

Published by Music Press Books
an imprint of John Blake Publishing Ltd
3 Bramber Court, 2 Bramber Road,
London W14 9PB, England

www.johnblakebooks.com

www.facebook.com/johnblakebooks f
twitter.com/jblakebooks t

First published in paperback in 2016

ISBN: 978 1 78606 015 0

British Library Cataloguing-in-Publication Data:

A catalogue record for this book is available from the British Library.

Design by www.envydesign.co.uk

Printed in Great Britain by CPI Group (UK) Ltd

3 5 7 9 10 8 6 4 2

Papers used by John Blake Publishing are natural, recyclable products made
from wood grown in sustainable forests. The manufacturing processes
conform to the environmental regulations of the country of origin.

Every attempt has been made to contact the relevant copyright-holders,
but some were unobtainable. We would be grateful if the appropriate
people could contact us.

To Katherine. No one else. Just Katherine.

ACKNOWLEDGEMENTS

Photographs and images by John Berry, Paul Burgess Archive, Ian Cartwright, Rachel Joseph, Peter Oldham, Andrew Orlowski, Cathryn Ormrod, Phil Singleton and Paul Welsh. For interviews and content, thanks to Gary Ainsley, Wayne Barrett, Howard Bates, John Berry, Will Birch, Dawn Bradbury, Steve 'Shy' Burke, Gordon Burns, Vanessa Corley, Howard Devoto, Steve Diggle, Dave Eyre, Eddie Garrity, Iain Grey, Phil Griffin, Alan Hempsall, Neal Holden, Peter Hook, Dave Howard, Jordan, Lorraine Joyce, Howard Kingston, John Maher, Terry Mason, Glen Matlock, Ian Moss, Paul Morley, NWA, Peter Oldham, Chris Pye, Mick Rossi, Pete Shelley, Phil Singleton, Mark E. Smith, Bernard Sumner, Peter Walker, Paul Welsh and Dick Witts. Some folks are sadly no longer with us: thank you Jon 'The Postman' Ormrod, Malcolm McLaren, and Tony Wilson.

Lucy Atkinson, Julian Coleman and especially Richard Makinson can swear they were there first time round, Martin Roach squared up for round two and the Italian version, but this time it's down to James Hodgkinson.

There are good people out there in punk rock land – Phil Singleton at sex-pistols.net, Paul 'Satellite' Burgess and Moz Murray are top of the pile, along with Matthew Norman at MDMA, Dave Gibson and Mick Wilkinson.

Thanks to all the authors and journalists who have credited *I Swear I Was There* over the years. As for those who should have but didn't...

CONTENTS

FOREWORD

A hundred or so punters turn up and Malcolm's quite pleased with me. Not too bad for 50p on a Friday evening. Inside, they like the Pistols all the way. The demand for an encore is insistent, even if they didn't get 'Woolly Bully' like some wag keeps shouting for. 'This is called "Problems". Where do you all come from?'

Johnny Rotten is being friendly back.

Were some of the assembled on their feet by the start of the second encore? Can't remember. But there's a delay and Glen Matlock is saying into a mic something about the guitarist needing to change a guitar string.

'Who caaaaares?!' someone yells. See? They've already got the idea. Well, one of the ideas.

Ideas.

Six weeks later. Tuesday. £1. Me and Pete Shelley have

finally got our band together. I've scribbled the Buzzcocks' set-list on the inside cover of one of my Castaneda books. Now it's come to it, I've realised I'm not up to stubbing cigarettes out on my body like Johnny reputedly does sometimes. And I had been planning to wash out a dog food tin, fill it with Fray Bentos pie filling and eat it on stage with a fork to bait Slaughter and the Dogs. Hadn't got round to that either somehow.

Now the Pistols are due on. I stick my head round their dressing room door.

'You ready?'

'Fuck off,' Johnny snarls at me.

Oh, right.

Howard Devoto

'Price 50p': A poster for the Sex Pistols at the Lesser Free Trade Hall, Manchester, 4 June 1976.   © *Paul Burgess Archive*

CHAPTER ONE

NOT ENTIRELY LOATH TO A BIT OF PROG ROCK

I'm not a great one for foreplay so let's get straight to it, shall we? Thousands of people claim to have attended the Sex Pistols gig at the Lesser Free Trade Hall in Manchester on 4 June 1976 – the gig named by the *NME* as the most important musical event of all time. But how many were really there? How many people splashed out to see a group of virtually unknown London lads playing a few tunes in a small, upstairs hall on Peter Street on a Friday night in Manchester all those years ago?

Well, as a great man once said, you can prove anything with facts. And records held in the archives of Manchester City Council couldn't be clearer in terms of clearing up one of rock music's great mysteries. The records show that £14 was generated in ticket sales – and at 50p a pop, that means that just twenty eight tickets were sold.

Not many for a show that has since been named by the *NME* as the greatest gig of all time. Modest for a concert celebrated in films like *24 Hour Party People* and *Control*. Pitiful, given that half the population of Greater Manchester lays claim to attendance.

Because this is *that* gig, the *famous* gig, the one that *everyone* claims to have been at – dare I say it – the *I Swear I Was There* gig. Famed not so much for the quality of the performance dished out by the Pistols that night but by the reaction of the audience that would spark a series of musical and pop-culture detonations that are still delighting and annoying people in equal measure today. As Sex Pistols' singer John Lydon (Johnny Rotten) would later point out, 'In Manchester, you'd play to half-empty halls but they'd all be there with *notepads*.'

TONY WILSON (audience member/TV presenter/Factory Records founder): Manchester was the fertile breeding ground, the field was ready-ploughed, ready-tilled, just ready to receive these seeds. It was the perfect punk city. The history of rock 'n' roll is the history of small cities.

GLEN MATLOCK (bass guitar – Sex Pistols): We never saw ourselves as a punk band. We hated the term punk. We were the Sex Pistols.

PETER HOOK (audience member/Joy Division/New Order): It was absolutely bizarre. It was the most shocking thing I've ever seen in my life, it was just unbelievable. We just looked at each other and thought My God! They [Sex Pistols] looked like they were having such a fantastic time. It was so ... alien to everything. You just thought, God ... we could do that! And I still to this day can't imagine why on earth we thought we could do that, 'cause I'd never played a musical instrument.

STEVE DIGGLE (audience member/Buzzcocks): That was the day the punk-rock atom was split, no doubt about it. The Pistols were glamorous and they didn't give a fuck. You got that vibe and the music was twice as fast as anything. It was amazing to see. That's where it exploded from, it changed Manchester and it changed the world.

Because *I Swear I Was There* is not a story about the Sex Pistols but a portrait of an audience booted into action by their response to four young men playing a few cover versions and some self-penned garage tunes. It's also a tale of myth-making on a grand scale; a series of escalating fibs and exaggerations that have become so potent that they've been accepted as fact for decades. Many tall tales have developed over the years about the 4 June gig, the Pistols' second appearance at the Lesser Free Trade Hall six weeks later and the band's first ever television appearance at Granada Television some five hundred yards down the road. Because of these myths, another great thing about this period is the lovely Mancunian cattiness that surrounds the whole story. I was there ... he wasn't ... she was there ... they *definitely* weren't there. One interviewee was asked if

Simply Red's Mick Hucknall was at the Lesser Free Trade Hall on that first night. 'I didn't see no Charlie Drake lookalikes,' he replied.

One of the other myths surrounding the Sex Pistols is that they hardly played any gigs – either because they couldn't actually play or because they were forever being banned by local councils. In fact, the first incarnation of the Sex Pistols played 124 gigs before they imploded in an onstage, premeditated tizz at the Winterland Ballroom in San Francisco on 14 January 1978.

But, of those 124 gigs, the most important were the 27th and the 36th. The two gigs they played at the Lesser Free Trade Hall in Manchester in the achingly hot summer of 1976. Because these gigs inspired a new shape for rock - a new way to pick it up and a new way to run with it. What came out of the two gigs at the Lesser Free Trade Hall in Manchester in 1976 became a blueprint for the UK music scene that has stood us in good stead for forty years. Not punk-a-likes, sound-a-likes or spike-a-likes, not suburban boredom clones and public schoolboys faking angst, but new music; post-punk music with legs that would influence bands across the country and then throughout the world.

Without gigs number twenty seven and thirty six there would be no Buzzcocks, Magazine, Joy Division, New Order, Factory Records, no 'indie' scene, no Fall, Smiths, Haçienda, Madchester, Happy Mondays or Oasis. Think then about the ripples of inspiration that came as a result of the bands and situations that sprang from those Pistols' gigs. Maybe there would be no Nirvana or Green Day, no Suede, no Killers, no Arctic Monkeys, no Editors or Interpol, no Blur, no Pavement, no Radiohead, no Prodigy, no Arcade Fire – all acts that owe a debt to bands formed in the sticky-carpeted aisles of the Lesser Free Trade Hall.

PAUL MORLEY (audience member/writer): Funnily enough, I've often done it for practice: join the line from the Sex Pistols all the way up to Mr Scruff and Badly Drawn Boy. Everything that happens is still a fall-out of the Sex Pistols coming to the Lesser Free Trade Hall. There's no doubt about it – all the way through Joy Division to The Stone Roses, from The Fall to Happy Mondays, all the way through to the dance stuff, anything mad that happened at The Haçienda, you can draw it all back to that little explosion at the Lesser Free Trade Hall. It's not hard at all.

Without the Sex Pistols gig on 4 June 1976, we would still be listening to everything and anything that the mid-1970s had to offer. And we all know what that entailed: leaden, overwrought and overlong public-school rock, faceless disco-dance music and pretty-boy assembly-line pop groups aimed at the pink and pubescent markets. Thankfully, that kind of nonsense could never rear its collectively unpleasant head again – could it? Of course not...

Today, there's actually very little to show for this most famous of musical events: a handmade poster, some Super 8mm film, a few snatched photographs from the audience and, of course, a ticket. The date printed on it is actually '4th June 1076'. It claimed to be for Sex Pistols '+ Buzzcocks'. It stated that it would 'admit one'. On the admittance front, that much, at least, is correct. The ticket did what it said – it admitted one. The rest of the ticket details – like so many aspects of our story – are wrong.

That aside, it is, indeed, a ticket for the Sex Pistols, live at the Lesser Free Trade Hall in Manchester, 4 June 1976. It's a ticket to see Johnny Rotten, Steve Jones, Glen Matlock and Paul Cook – young men barely out of their teens – perform live on stage. The date stamped on the ticket (1076) is 900 years out of whack, thanks to some careless hand-printing by the promoters. No matter. In a way, the mistakes make it all the more special.

It is a noteworthy ticket for the first of two gigs that changed the world. Buzzcocks never actually got their act together to play at the first one. The band that actually appeared in their place is one of a hundred stories you're about to read. You'll find out who was there, who wasn't there, and what they went on to do. You'll also see pictures and memories that have never been seen or heard before about those three events during the summer of 1976: the two gigs and that first ever television appearance.

Who told a handful of young, hirsute Mancunians to 'Fuck off out of it'? Who threw peanuts at Slaughter And The Dogs? Who called Clive James a 'Baldie old Sheila'? And who the hell are Gentlemen?

All in good time.

Sex Pistols did not elect to come to Manchester – Manchester invited Sex Pistols to come to it and for that we can thank two young men who shared a mutual dissatisfaction with the music that was being offered to them at their college in the north of England. Peter McNeish and Howard Trafford were, essentially, responsible for everything that is about to unfold: two students who, after seeing the Pistols twice in February 1976, helped change the face of music – the way we access it, the manner in which we dance to it and the extent to which we will pursue it. And that, brothers and sisters, means that this gig changed the world. While all this was going on, these two students changed their names as well, to Pete Shelley and Howard Devoto.

HOWARD DEVOTO (singer – Buzzcocks/Magazine): I spent my early childhood in the Midlands and then my teenage years in Leeds, so those were the years the hormones hit. My first ever love was The Shadows. After that I liked The Rolling Stones and after that I liked Bob Dylan, I liked Jimi Hendrix ... things like The Mothers of Invention and then David Bowie. I went to college, the Bolton Institute of Technology, in 1972, messed around trying to do a Psychology degree for a year and a half, packed that up, went back and did a Humanities degree. This brings us to the more pertinent years. What I always remember of my time then really is buying *Fun House* [1970] by The Stooges. I didn't really know any Stooges' fans and their records were very hard to get hold of, although *Raw Power* had come out in 1973 and I did manage to get a copy at the local record shop in Bolton. That was about it. Then I managed to pick up a second-hand copy of their first album [*The Stooges*, 1969] from somewhere or other. But

Fun House was proving quite hard to track down. I wasn't quite sure I liked The Stooges that much. I liked the story, I liked the legend but, for me, *Raw Power* was a bit messy and the first Stooges' album was a little simplistic. But then when I finally managed to get an import copy of *Fun House* it all fell into place. It just kind of hit me at the time when I was starting to get really pissed off again in life. I have this memory of myself at this place I was living – an ex-convent that had been taken over for student accommodation – in my room playing *Fun House* and loving the primitive nature and anger. I really connected with it and started thinking, 'I could just about do this.'

PETE SHELLEY (singer – Buzzcocks): Albums by Yes were getting longer and longer ... longer than most people's entire recorded output.

TONY WILSON: It's hard to describe how bloody awful music was, how desperately bad it was, how our Sixties heroes had become boring and useless and how the stuff that was happening then was ... not only was it bad, they were *badly dressed*. The only music I was listening to in late 1975 was Austin, Texas country music. The rest of it was a wasteland of boredom and [TV show] *The Old Grey Whistle Test*. Between Christmas and New Year [1975– 76] a kid called Dennis Brown who was a deadhead from university, a mate of mine, gave me the Patti Smith *Horses* album. God, it was fantastic and different and wonderful.

MARK E. SMITH (lead singer – The Fall): I was

working on the docks at the time and I wasn't long out of school. The stuff I used to like was mid-Sixties American trash bands ... garage stuff like The Seeds, The Stooges, things like that. A bit of trashy soul, dub reggae. I didn't like anything that was out at the time. You just weren't interested really – a bit like now. Radio was a no-no. At the time, I thought the best Manchester band was probably The Hollies ... or Freddie And The Dreamers. We were doing poetry to guitars, but we were doing it in our flat. Someone would read a poem out – we had a bass player who was into [jazz musician and Weather Report member] Jaco Pastorius – it was very much influenced by Patti Smith. You didn't think of actually attempting to play live. You had to have a drummer and lights, all that sort of thing.

STEVE DIGGLE: I am strictly Manchester. Can't get more central than St Mary's Hospital on Upper Brook Street. I'm probably the only Mancunian in Buzzcocks. Shelley was a woollyback from Leigh, Howard was from Leeds or something. I was born at St Mary's Hospital on 10 May 1955, the year of rock 'n' roll. My dad used to work for [Moors Murderer] Ian Brady's stepfather as a decorator. It turned out he made a name for himself, Ian Brady. So there's that connection, that's before The Smiths thought about such things. My mum had a clothes shop on Stockport Road. Lived there till age seven, clothes business went bust, and then we moved to Bradford. Anybody that knows Manchester proper knows there's a Bradford in Manchester. *Coronation Street*, y'know? I remember walking down and seeing all the street gangs. We had a street army, a street football team and a street newspaper for a while. My mate who lived in the street, we both said we'd never do anything with our lives. He became a brain surgeon and I became a musician with Buzzcocks.

PAUL MORLEY: Stockport Technical College had two or three gigs a year. Elton John came when I was thirteen, which just seemed like manna from heaven. It was just the most extraordinary thing. They wouldn't have groups play there, but they would often have film of groups playing. I remember they had a film of Jimi Hendrix, which was the biggest thing that happened in 1975.

PAMELA ROOKE AKA JORDAN (shop assistant/punk muse): I come from a place near Brighton which was really quite a hip place – a lot of great clubs there, usually gay clubs. They're still bands that I really love – Iggy Pop, Lou Reed, David Bowie – I guess quite a lot of people say that was what they were listening to early on, before the Pistols, before punk. I think people see that as the grounding really for punk.

JON THE POSTMAN (Jonathan Ormrod – audience member): In 1976 I was twenty and I was a postman, which I had been since 1972. We were punks before punk ... in our heads anyway. We just didn't have an outlet for it. I had been buying records since I was seven years of age. I had been listening to that sort of music since 1970. Mid-

Sixties garage stuff, The Velvet Underground, The Stooges, the MC5. Plus the horrible stuff that was happening at the time. The arse-end of prog rock. I used to buy stuff in 1975, early 1976, but I wasn't that enthusiastic.

IAN MOSS (audience member): You can never just say *everything* was a load of rubbish. But there was a lot of rubbish ... really hideous, a lot of it. And disgusting. And pompous. And American.

MICK ROSSI (guitarist – Slaughter And The Dogs): Any good band, they're going to have *Ziggy Stardust* [in their record collection], they're going to have [Lou Reed's] *Transformer*, they're going to have *Slaughter On 10th Avenue* [by Mick Ronson], they're going to have Marc Bolan records there. It's just a great grounding for anyone, those records.

GLEN MATLOCK: The glam-rock thing was over. There had been a pub-rock thing which hadn't really made it. Bands like Yes and Barclay James Harvest didn't really touch the kids in the street around my way. Punk was something that kids could identify with and get their teeth into. Everybody was looking for something at the same time. We was there because we was just that little bit ahead of the game. We were like the standard bearers for the movement and everybody else rallied around us. When we came up to Manchester and started playing around a bit, we had a little bit of press by then. We'd already got an inkling of, you know, here's something new. So we came with a bit more of an open mind about it than maybe we'd had when we'd been doing some little club in London.

The punk-rock musical touchstones from this time tend to be a shared experience, at least publicly. The same names occur: The Stooges, the MC5, New York Dolls, Lou Reed, Patti Smith, Roxy Music, David Bowie and bands that made it onto Elektra Records' *Nuggets* compilation album in 1972, such as The Standells and ? & The Mysterians. A bit of good-time glam falls easily into the mix too: the hairy-chested camp of Sweet, Gary Glitter and Slade. But what about more primitive UK influences like the bare bones R'n'B of Dr Feelgood, formed in 1971, and the shouty power-pop of Eddie And The Hot Rods, who came together four years later? Perhaps because they all came bearing the unfashionable beer-brown stain of what was, by this time in 1976, last month's thing – pub rock.

WILL BIRCH (musician/author – *No Sleep Till Canvey Island, The Great Pub Rock Revolution*): Dr Feelgood and Eddie And The Hot Rods did have influence over the punk-rock groups. The speed at which they took the music and their onstage aggression was inherited. The Feelgoods and the Hot Rods primed the audience for the Sex Pistols and The Clash. There was a young audience, mainly eighteen-year-old blokes who had seen them and bought *Stupidity* [Dr Feelgood's third album, 1976] and *Teenage Depression* [Eddie And The Hot Rods, 1976].

When the Sex Pistols came along it was, 'Hey, yeah, we're ready for this.' I'm not so sure so many people would have been ready to embrace the Sex Pistols had it not been for that groundwork.

PAUL MORLEY: I'd been interested in pop music and I'd fallen in love with Marc Bolan when I was young, but I was also interested in all sorts of stranger kinds of music, things like The Velvet Underground and The Stooges and strange German alternative music, free jazz. Patti Smith had just happened and that front cover of *Horses* with a black-and-white shot that Robert Mapplethorpe did with the skinny tie and the white shirt ... it seemed so full of colour and life, even though it was monochrome. Dr Feelgood seemed incredibly relevant, because the songs were short and sharp and fast and ferocious and angry ... and seemed to be cutting away all the fat and flab and artificiality that there was elsewhere in the more commercial record company types of music. And The Ramones had just happened from New York.

JON THE POSTMAN: The MC5? ... I mean they were playing a similar sort of music but they didn't have the attitude ... you know, 'Fuck you'. I mean, they were actually involved in the optimistic hippy time, they weren't like totally nihilistic like the Pistols.

HOWARD DEVOTO: I was not totally loath to a little bit of prog rock. I do remember going along to the college gigs every Saturday night, but really getting very fed up with it and feeling, I wish I could go and see The Stooges or something like that, something that's really going to be confrontational and aggressive and exciting and a bit dangerous.

STEVE DIGGLE: I remember seeing The Who at Belle Vue Kings Hall. I saw Status Quo there as well and that was great. I saw Led Zeppelin. I even liked Yes songs. But it just became irrelevant. Prog rock didn't fit into the backdrop really, because it was coming up to a million people on the dole. I think our generation was questioning their lives, rather than wanting to be entertained.

EDDIE GARRITY (singer – Ed Banger And The Nosebleeds): Well, I was a big Slade fan at the time so I was following them by the time they came along. But anything with Roxy, anything like that or Bowie ... more the harder edge sort of bands.

TONY WILSON: At that time you've got John Miles, the guitarist, you get Be-Bop Deluxe, you get Eddie And The Hot Rods, who were kind of a pop pre-cursor to punk.

PAUL MORLEY: At the beginning of 1976 I was eighteen and turned nineteen just before the Sex Pistols came up to Manchester. I know it sounds crazy now but at the time we were still coming out of the war, it was still a bleak kind of time and we'd just come out of the three-day week and life was a lot more minimal and sparse. Sparser than it is now, when it's so full of stimulation and signs of pop culture. Back then it was very raw and naked. And so, even though I was eighteen, nineteen ... it would have been fourteen, fifteen in today's terms. You were still kind of trying to find a way to rebel. There wasn't processed rebellion, the rebellion wasn't packaged like it is now and marketed to segments of teen life. It was something you discovered for yourself. Looking back, I think of myself as being very young – I'm surprised how kind of naïve I was in a way. But I was definitely trying to find something out for myself that would help me, rather than what I was being told was the way forward.

STEVE DIGGLE: I used to live in a house where lots of people were taking acid and questioning things. We'd trip all night, take acid and figure things out. We were worried about going to the shop for a loaf of bread in case the 'normals' influenced you. Some ended up in Prestwich Mental Hospital. I tried to get a band together, but everyone was tripping so I realised it was a waste of time.

HOWARD DEVOTO: I started the second year of my course. I'd had a slightly unfortunate encounter with exams – I didn't do that brilliantly in my first year – so when I went into the second year of my course, I was kind of looking round for other things to get involved with and one of the things I did was to stick up a notice at college asking to meet musicians. I mentioned the name of The Stooges in the advert and 'Sister Ray' [by The Velvet Underground] and stuff like this. Possibly, Pete [Shelley] was the only person who answered that advert. No, he wasn't the *only* person but he was the only person I kind of stuck with. We'd been trying things with a drummer ... some Stooges songs, trying some [Brian] Eno songs, even trying some early Rolling Stones songs. But it really was not happening. So by February 1976, I don't think we really knew where any of this was going, except that we were vaguely still trying to get a band together.

Peter McNeish [Shelley] was from Leigh, near Wigan, one of scores of towns that hover around Manchester like satellites. Although he was three years younger than Howard Devoto, McNeish was way ahead of him in terms of organisation. He had already been involved with bands at Leigh Grammar School. The bands were called Kogg and then Jets Of Air and dated back as far as 1971. He learned how to hire halls, how to play gigs and he actually made money. These were entrepreneurial skills that were about to be put into very good use.

PETE SHELLEY: We're to blame for lots of things! We were quite strange, Jets Of Air. As well as my own songs, we used to do Roxy Music, Velvet Underground and David Bowie covers. It was hard to get gigs really. There was always the pub-rock circuit but you had to play songs that people knew, basically do like a 'living juke box'. Most of the gigs we did were ones which we organised ourselves, so I'd go and hire a local hall and sell tickets. The money used to balance out. If you overestimate the cost and underestimate the profit and if you could still make it break even, then you're on a sure-fire winner. So it was just a case of trying to find places to play. We even played a Christian Society party at Bolton Grammar School, which was strange.

HOWARD DEVOTO: Pete claims that the Jets Of Air came from some kind of phrase he got in a chemistry or physics lesson. I believe him...

Howard and Pete's Bolton Bohemia consisted of very few things that would actually contribute to the formation of a band, apart from a lot of album listening. Howard would on occasion buy entire back catalogues of bands he favoured from second-hand shops.

HOWARD DEVOTO: John Cale [Velvet Underground], his solo albums. *Fear* [1974] was a really important record to me. Then I did discover The Velvet Underground very late. Eno songs were among the earliest we would sort of practise with. We'd even try to perform. So there was a sort of contingent of people that seemed to be kind of interesting before the Patti Smiths. One was reading about all that was happening in New York but you couldn't hear any of it.

If New York seemed a world away, London appeared only marginally closer to the boys from the Bolton Institute. Their best points of access to the capital and the UK and

American scenes were weekly musical missives in the form of the 'inkies' – the British music press. One springtime article in particular caught the eye of both Trafford and McNeish: a review about a band supporting Eddie And The Hot Rods at London's Marquee club. The piece would take them across the country. It changed their names and it changed their lives, according to Howard, 'beyond a room full of shadows of doubt.' It inspired them to put on the gig that changed the world.

HOWARD DEVOTO: *New Musical Express* came out in Bolton and I kind of flipped through it and gave it to Pete. He looked through it and handed it back to me and said, 'Did you read that?' and this was the first ever review of the Sex Pistols by Neil Spencer [*New Musical Express*, 12 February 1976] ... DON'T LOOK OVER YOUR SHOULDER BUT THE SEX PISTOLS ARE COMING. The Stooges were mentioned in there and 'We're not into music, we're into chaos'. There was that line in there. Well, it clicked with me and it just so happened I could borrow a car that weekend. I didn't have a car, but somebody in the house I was living in at that time had asked me to pick up their car and said, 'You can borrow it for the weekend.' I don't think they meant, 'You can drive to London for the weekend...' But anyway, that's what Pete and I ended up doing. Just on the basis of reading this review and the fact that I could borrow this car. It was the weekend that changed our lives.

MALCOLM MCLAREN (manager – Sex Pistols): Howard was a guy, I think, that picked up on a small article in the *NME* about the Sex Pistols ... and how dreadful they were.

McLaren was a shopkeeper. The store he ran with Vivienne Westwood at 430 King's Road, Chelsea in London had previously been a supplier of New Edwardian – or Teddy Boy – gear called Let It Rock, later renamed, Too Fast to Live, Too Young to Die. By the time Shelley and Devoto arrived at his shop in search of the Sex Pistols, it was billed as being run by 'Specialists in rubberwear, glamourwear and stagewear' and went by the name of Sex. McLaren had jettisoned the retro style of the old shop in favour of the 'Sex' look after a trip to New York, where he came across a band that couldn't play too well but had a knockout image: the New York Dolls.

The origins of the band that would partly bear the shop's name – the Sex Pistols – go back as early as 1972, as a schoolboy band in Shepherd's Bush. It featured Steve Jones (vocals), Paul Cook (drums) and Warwick 'Wally' Nightingale (guitar) under the name of The Strand, a seemingly compulsory early 1970s nod to Roxy Music.

PHIL SINGLETON (creator of sex-pistols.net): Steve Jones was certainly a thief and a criminal, driven to that by his background, by poverty, by neglect. He used to witness his mother stealing. He didn't have a role model really, other than one of survival.

When not stealing the best equipment money could buy, Jones was a King's Road regular and enthusiastic shoplifter from McLaren's shop. Despite this, McLaren found them rehearsal space and a bass player, Glen Matlock. Wally changed the name of the group to the decidedly proto-punk Swankers and set upon drilling the band through a series of mod cover versions and faltering originals for nearly a year. Nightingale was replaced soon afterwards after turning up at a rehearsal to find Jones had taken over as guitarist. By 1975 John Lydon had been parachuted into the band as lead singer, a role Jones neither relished nor desired. In a neat piece of product placement, the new version of the band virtually shared a name with their manager's clothes shop, with a view to helping him sell his couture – or 'trousers', if you prefer. The Sex Pistols played their first gig with the newly named Johnny 'Rotten' on 6 November 1975 at St Martin's School of Art. There's a fake blue plaque there now to mark the occasion. Front of house at Sex was the living embodiment of the shop's ethos, Pamela Rooke – the shop assistant also known as Jordan.

JORDAN: I decided that, after I'd done my A Levels, I wanted to come up to London, with the purpose of working for Vivienne [Westwood] and Malcolm [McLaren] in their shop in King's Road. I got an interim job with Harrods with the hope that maybe I'd get a job at Vivienne's. I walked in one day and had a quite a long talk with the manager, and I guess he liked the way I looked and Malcolm liked the way I looked. A few days later I got called up and asked if I'd do an afternoon. That afternoon lasted for some years. Boy George used to come in the shop – he used to come to lots of gigs and buy a lot of clothes from Vivienne. He always seemed to have a lot of money ... [laughing] ... I'll have to ask him one day where he got it from.

HOWARD DEVOTO: We first met Malcolm when we turned up at Sex, his shop, having been told by Neil Spencer at the *New Musical Express* – who I'd phoned – that, 'Oh, I think their manager runs the Sex shop on King's Road.' So we were vaguely expecting to turn up to an Anne Summers-type shop.

JORDAN: I'd been, I suppose for want of a better description, the front person of Vivienne's shop. A lot of glossy girl magazines used to come and take photos and talk to me about what the shop was all about. I was dressing very crazy at that time, very Fifties ... bouffant, black eyeliner, sort of 'Cleopatra-goes-Fifties' ... with lots of ripped tights and stilettos and Perspex clothes. I was doing my own thing, buying my own clothes, down in Sussex, which were really comparable with what Malcolm and Vivienne were doing up in London. I commuted for about two years. I had some really bad do's on the train – I had tourists trying to pay me for my photo ... worse than that, mothers saying that I'm upsetting their children and debauching them and how dare I get on a train looking like that. Somebody tried to throw me off the train one day, literally out the door. So British Rail told me to go and sit in first class to get out of trouble. Me sitting on the train in my rubber gear and what have you, a few men used to get a bit het up as well. I think that might have caused a bit of a stir.

PETE SHELLEY: They said, 'There's this guy who's got this shop on the King's Road.' So we started off at Sloane Square and walked all the way down. Got there and they were just closing up. So we asked Malcolm and he said, 'Oh yeah, the boys are playing in High Wycombe.' We saw two shows that weekend and it was great. Howard was talking to Malcolm and Malcolm was saying that he wanted to have a gig outside of London 'cause all he could get was little gigs.

HOWARD DEVOTO: I remember Jordan was there, and Malcolm turned up a short while later, in his black leather stuff ... well, they're desperately cool, aren't they? So I don't expect anybody was going, 'Oh, wow ... you've come all the way down from Manchester to see us.'

PETE SHELLEY: I mean, we were from up North! They were wearing Vivienne Westwood clothes. We just made our own.

HOWARD DEVOTO: Malcolm turned up and of course, at that point we didn't even know whether they were playing – we'd come down totally on spec. We bought our copy of *Time Out*, where we get the name Buzzcocks from [a story about 1970s TV music show *Rock Follies*, which carried the headline IT'S THE BUZZ, COCK!). Can't find anything about them. When we finally meet Malcolm, we learn that, 'Oh yes, they are actually playing tonight and supporting Malcolm and Vivienne's mate Screaming Lord Sutch.'

JORDAN: When the Pistols came along, it seemed to come together really quickly. I used to go to rehearsals sometimes – I mean, that was pretty dodgy. I never had any doubt whatsoever. That old adage about the clothes and the music coming together – it was one of the first times in history where a look was actually created for a band that people could buy. I just knew they were going to do it: if they hadn't had those clothes, they would have still done it. If they hadn't had the Malcolm and the Vivienne ethic behind them, I think they would have still done it.

TONY WILSON: Malcolm wanted, in the Pistols, to create the Bay City Rollers of outrage. He wanted a band who couldn't play, who swore, who were just appalling ... and who would be Number 1 just 'cause they were disgusting. In fact, they became Number 1 because they were fantastic. Culturally ... musically, even. Malcolm, I always think, got screwed by art. He actually created a great artwork and he didn't really want that. He wanted to create something that was actually valueless and would make some kind of political joke. Instead, he got this great moment in cultural history.

JORDAN: Malcolm had a huge influence on the Pistols, but there's no way you could make somebody do those things. They had a positive attitude and it just seemed to bring the youth of the whole country together. Working in a shop in King's Road you would have people coming from absolutely everywhere to buy stuff there. It was a real treat; it was a pilgrimage down the King's Road.

HOWARD DEVOTO: Everything about the Sex Pistols impressed at that first gig we went to at High Wycombe [College of Higher Education, 20 February 1976] and the second one. They repeated the experience the following evening at Welwyn Garden City [21 February 1976]. Most importantly, the music. And for me, the lyrics. We could hear some interesting lyrics going on in there. The *aggro* of it was interesting. At that first gig, John [Johnny Rotten] got into a bit of a tussle with somebody in the audience and kept singing under a small pile of people. That was sort of what one had been looking for, for quite a while. He would get his hanky out and stick it up his nose and he'd wander off the stage for five minutes and then come back. Just right, spot on. Impressed. I mean, at that time, his look was a kind of skinhead look – but a different take on that. The ripped sweater – it was just different. Pete and I immediately had a model. When we saw the Pistols, we'd got a musical model.

PETE SHELLEY: They enjoyed the same kind of music that me and Howard liked. I mean, they were playing 'No

Fun' and we liked The Stooges. They were playing short, sharp songs. Even their version of 'Steppin' Stone' [most famously recorded by The Monkees] was a wonder to behold. We saw them doing it and we thought, 'Well, if they can do it, we can do it.' Howard and I decided that we would make it happen, rather than just writing songs and not do anything. So we worked towards making our dream a reality.

HOWARD DEVOTO: I went up to Malcolm after they'd played and said, 'If we could organise for you to play at our college, are you interested in coming up to do it?' And he said, 'Yeah, sure, if you can arrange it, we'll come up and do it.' I think the Pistols were kind of chuffed: 'Wow, you know, these guys have come all the way down from Manchester to see us.'

PETE SHELLEY: All the gigs they could get were basically within the M25, if it existed then – I don't know – but all it had been till then was just Greater London. It was the only place they could get gigs, so the idea was that, if we get something outside of London, at least it's onwards and upwards...

Howard Devoto and Pete Shelley – as they had now named themselves – returned home in their borrowed car. They were determined to bring the Sex Pistols north and for their new band – Buzzcocks – to act as support. The first problem was where to play. The obvious choice was their

27

own college. The Pistols' Manchester debut – the Gig That Changed The World, mind you – should have actually been at The Bolton Institute but the college's powers-that-be managed to talk themselves out of a place in rock history.

HOWARD DEVOTO: When Pete and I got back to college, despite Pete's clout in the Students' Union, they weren't going for it – not interested in putting them on. Malcolm might have said something like, 'We don't want to play a pub,' because, of course, pub rock was kind of the vibe that consciously or unconsciously people were trying to get away from. It might have been hippies and prog rock at a higher level, but at a lower level it was pub rock.

WILL BIRCH: When a lot of the punk-rock groups came out, they claimed to be influenced by the New York Dolls, The Stooges and the MC5. But none of those American groups sold very many records in the UK. So I think there was a little bit of bandwagon jumping in that respect. They did owe quite a lot to the preceding pub-rock era. What pub rock did, immediately before punk rock, was to establish a network of venues and infrastructure.

PHIL SINGLETON: With pub rock, a lot of it was still cover versions – although the Sex Pistols did their fair share of covers. So that's what you would go along in 1976 to see: a pub-rock band, doing pretty much what pub-rock bands do, which is a few naff self-penned songs and a few covers.

The venue that Shelley and Devoto ended up with was most definitely not a pub. The ornate Free Trade Hall on Peter Street was one of Manchester's largest theatres and played host to all the big bands of the day. It was also popular as a venue of presentation ceremonies for students receiving degrees. Above it was a mini-version, an all-seated auditorium, called the Lesser Free Trade Hall.

HOWARD DEVOTO: So when I phoned Malcolm and told him, 'They're not going for it,' he said, 'Well, see if you can find somewhere else ... then we'll come up and play.' We somehow learned about this little hall above the Free Trade Hall ... the Lesser Free Trade Hall. As if it's some kind of curious bird, you know, a 'lesser-spotted auditorium'. It was not a lot of money, so I got back to Malcolm again: 'Yeah, OK, hire it!' I made sure he sent me a cheque to cover the payment. So that first gig for 4 June 1976 was suddenly on the cards.

Despite having booked the Lesser Free Trade Hall, it became increasingly apparent that Devoto and Shelley's band would not be ready in time to support their London heroes.

HOWARD DEVOTO: Malcolm McLaren paid for the hall so it wasn't going to be a huge disaster if nobody turned up. The main thing that was bugging me and Pete was the fact that our bloody group wasn't ready.

PETE SHELLEY: We didn't have a bass player. Or a drummer. They were our sticking points.

HOWARD DEVOTO: We didn't know a load of musicians; we weren't on any musician circuit. It was just very, very difficult to find people. Just the usual problems you have when you've got no money and nowhere to rehearse. We just couldn't make it happen. I'm still at college, trying to be a promoter for the first time. Just arranging it for the Sex Pistols in itself was a really big thrill at that point in my life.

PETE SHELLEY: We were sticking up posters so that maybe more people would find out about the gig. But also the Sex Pistols were getting write-ups in music papers on a regular basis and so it seemed more and more people had heard that something was happening ... and they started checking it out.

Not wishing to embarrass themselves in front of McLaren and the Pistols, Devoto and Shelley stepped down as support act – despite the fact they'd already made the tickets with 'Buzzcocks' printed on them – and resigned themselves to the roles of promoters and organisers for the upcoming gig. The Free Trade Hall had been host to many legendary concerts but not many people knew of its little cousin up above, so promotion was going to vital if the gig was going to be a success.

PETE SHELLEY: The Lesser Free Trade Hall is up the stairs. It's usually used for lectures before classical concerts: 'Go in, find out what Beethoven really meant.' It was just available for hire. It held about three hundred people.

Pete Shelley may believe it was 'just available for hire' but others can throw a harsher light on the history of the building.

PHIL GRIFFIN (writer on architecture): It's on the site of the Peterloo Massacre [a political reform rally that ended with a charge by the military – eleven people died, literally, by the sword]. It is, after all, the only civic building that I know that's named after a radical political movement ... the Free Trade Movement, the Anti-Corn Law League. *Italianate* is what people tend to call it. Architect? David Walters, 1853. A high Victorian respect for Italian buildings is what it demonstrates. As with a lot of buildings at the time, it's all front. It's always been a place where young people and audiences have gathered in order to express themselves in one way or another. Until very recently, it's been a place for trade-union meetings. There's many a strike been voted for in the Free Trade Hall. There's certainly been a history of radicalism in terms of its performance. I'm referring to the famous 1965 concert when a member of the audience at the Manchester Free Trade Hall – not the Albert Hall, as many believe – accused Bob Dylan of being 'Judas'. Strong words, in my view. I was there that night and gradually the Free Trade Hall emptied. The first set was acoustic and familiar, then on marched these people who the audience hadn't invited, making noises they weren't familiar with. They got most upset about it. People even write books about it.

PAUL MORLEY: The Manchester Free Trade Hall was like this cathedral of conventional, established sounds. You'd see your Pink Floyds and your David Bowies and your T. Rexes and so that was incredibly exciting. But the Sex Pistols played the *Lesser* Free Trade Hall ... this sort of part of the Free Trade that you didn't know anything about. In fact, the only time I'd come across the Lesser Free Trade Hall before is when some theatre company had done a performance of *Waiting for Godot*, where they all acted it out as members of the IRA. So, the idea that the Sex Pistols were playing there, that was also incredibly kind of unusual.

MARK E. SMITH (audience member – lead singer, The Fall): The Free Trade Hall was ... not sacred ... it was like so crap. I'd been to a few shows there ... most of the bands that are coming back now. It's like a time warp for me.

PAUL MORLEY: It was a very shrewd choice by Howard Devoto to put them on there, because it could have just been a grungy little dirty club or somewhere difficult to get to. Because it was the Lesser Free Trade Hall, you kind of knew how to get to it. I know that sounds strange, but I mean, for a long time, I thought underground music was something that genuinely happened underground, that you couldn't go to unless you looked a certain way, smelt a certain way and dressed a certain way. So the fact that it was at the Lesser Free Trade Hall, that made it very accessible ... Oh, I can get to that, I know how to get tickets for the Lesser Free Trade Hall ... you just go to the box office. So the whole thing had this kind of fantastic mystery and distance, but also seemed very close.

JOHN BERRY (audience member): We didn't even know where the Lesser Free Trade Hall was – we'd never heard of it. We knew the Free Trade Hall – we'd been to loads of concerts there. We didn't know the Lesser Free Trade Hall even existed.

By late May 1976 Howard Devoto and Pete Shelley were doing everything in their power to make sure as many people as possible managed to find their way to the gig. Like so many would-be promoters before and after them, they found themselves wandering around a British city centre late at night with a sheath of posters and a bucket full of wallpaper paste.

HOWARD DEVOTO: McLaren certainly sent up some A3 posters that he'd got printed off. Malcolm was quite good with Jamie Reid [situationist partner-in-crime of McLaren and instigator of the 'blackmail' style of lettering common to a lot of Pistols/punk artwork] 'cause of his background in putting together press packs, which did have a fairly strong design element. The thing that impressed us about them was that they put in all the bad reviews as well. Pete and I were suddenly in the fly-poster business. We did go up and down Oxford Road [the main road through Manchester's student area] pasting these A3 things, which, at the end of the day, were trying to double up as leaflets and posters. They weren't very imposing and whether they managed to pull in anybody, I've no idea. At the end of May, probably barely a week before the first gig, a cassette tape turned up [with Pistols' demos]. We thought they sounded great. I copied the cassette onto my reel-to-reel, 'cause I wasn't advanced enough to have a cassette player. I can't remember quite what my contact with Tony Wilson was but I got this tape to him.

Tony Wilson was a Salford-born Cambridge graduate who was several years into his career in television. After working as a trainee at ITN in London, he returned north to Granada Television, where he was a reporter and presenter for *Granada Reports*. This was the teatime news-magazine programme that served the north-west of England, an area of the country known at the time as *Granadaland*. As a presenter on the news – and the new *So It Goes* music-and-arts programme – Wilson had developed a sarky, ironic style that seemed designed to wind audiences up. At home, my parents always referred to him as 'That Tony Wilson'.

Although a hippie at heart, Wilson knew that musical change was in the air when he started to get strange things in the mail at his desk at Granada Television's studios on

Quay Street in Manchester, just a few hundred yards from the Lesser Free Trade Hall. Wilson was a jack-of-all-trades in telly terms, perfectly able to front a political piece as well as an 'and finally' item. But what he really wanted to do was a full-on music, comedy and arts show. And he'd just received the green light.

TONY WILSON: I sat around in those first six months waiting to do this 'comedy show', bored shitless by the bands. Then two things happened to me. One: I got one of those Wilton packaging, brown cardboard LP sleeves. Inside it was this battered copy of the New York Dolls' album ... just the cover. No vinyl with it. I presume Mozzer kept his vinyl at home. The note was from this Stretford schoolboy called Steven Morrissey [later lead singer of The Smiths] saying, 'Why can't there be more bands like this?' Then I got this cassette through the post, saying, 'Dear Mr Wilson...' It was from someone called Howard Trafford. He said there's a new band from London, they're coming to Manchester on 4 June, I think you'll like them. I've still got the cassette box, but someone nicked the tape. I think one of the tracks was 'Pretty Vacant'.

HOWARD DEVOTO: I had no idea who Tony Wilson was. Somehow or other I got in touch with Tony and I got this tape to him. That's the degree of contact really that I remember. It's the same degree that I remember with Malcolm. I did meet up with him briefly when I went down to see Bowie play at the Empire Pool, Wembley.

Malcolm looked down his nose at that. The main thing that was going on at that time in the music press was the mentions of the Sex Pistols getting more and more frequent. I'm not quite sure at what point they made the front page of *Melody Maker*, but their profile was building in the music papers.

TONY WILSON: In May [1976] I'd gone to The Roundhouse in London. We couldn't get a permit to film Patti Smith but I was able to at least interview her. She was having PMT at the time so it was a bloody nightmare. Hanging around waiting for her all afternoon in The Roundhouse, I sat in some side room with this young *NME* journalist. It was Tony Parsons. We sat there, swinging our legs at this table, and he was telling me about this band I was going to see in two weeks' time – the Pistols. He thought they were fantastic. So, yes, there's this swell all the way throughout that first six months of 1976 ... of maybe something happening. It's hard to remember now that we're used to continuous rebirth in pop music, that however bad it gets ... it will get exciting again. That first time, it might never have got exciting again, it might never have changed. Which is why, sitting in that old theatre seat on 4 June and watching this Pistols thing was such a shock. I'm very lucky, I was at the first one. Because the first one was utterly and painfully outrageous and wonderful ... I'm Gig One.

PETE SHELLEY: We found out we could hire the Lesser Free Trade Hall for about thirty two pounds or something. Just doing the maths we knew that, if we got forty people in, we would be in profit, so it seemed like a good idea.

Buzzcocks did manage a gig of sorts, two months before the Pistols' Manchester gig. They played songs by David Bowie and The Rolling Stones. Badly.

HOWARD DEVOTO: The debut of an entity called Buzzcocks actually took place on 1 April at The Bolton Institute of Technology.

PETE SHELLEY: A complete disaster. I think there were three songs. The first song lasted about twenty minutes ... even though it wasn't supposed to. There were things borrowed and stolen but part of it was just getting back to short songs and the more direct delivery ... just making music exciting again. It's a bit like riding a bike ... take off your stabilisers and give yourself a big push and hope for the best.

HOWARD DEVOTO: I was there at the gig in my new drainpipes and knee-length pink boots, feeling very splendid.

PETE SHELLEY: Howard went to a boutique and chose a pair of trousers and said he wanted them altering. He said, 'Well, I want them taking in,' because everything was flares. So he had them taken in so they were almost like drainpipes ... and the guy said, 'Are you sure about this? Because after it's done, they won't be able to stitch it back together. You've ruined the trousers.' Howard could stop traffic by walking in tight trousers – it was amazing.

HOWARD DEVOTO: I think we might have played 'Oh Shit!' ... 'No Reply' ... 'Get On Our Own', things like that. We hadn't written any co-compositions like 'Breakdown' ... 'Time's Up' ... certainly not 'Boredom'. We got the plug pulled on us after three numbers.

PETE SHELLEY: It meant that, instead of thinking about doing it, we'd actually done it. Because, if you think about doing things, there's always problems and you're trying to think of ways of solving that problem, even though the problem may never arise, so by doing things ... you actually get them done, not by thinking about it. You have to think about them to a certain extent but at some point you have to trust the fact that you are going to do it.

So, flushed with failure from their first gig, not to mention cold, sticky and smelling a little odd after their nocturnal fly-posting missions, Pete and Howard returned home. Rather charmingly, the pair were now living just a few doors away from each other on Lower Broughton Road in Salford, the city that sits back-to-back with Manchester. Despite all the setbacks, the idea of the Sex Pistols – and indeed, punk rock – was becoming a reality and spreading swiftly across the city of Manchester. News of the gig was also making in-roads, perhaps even more importantly, into the suburbs.

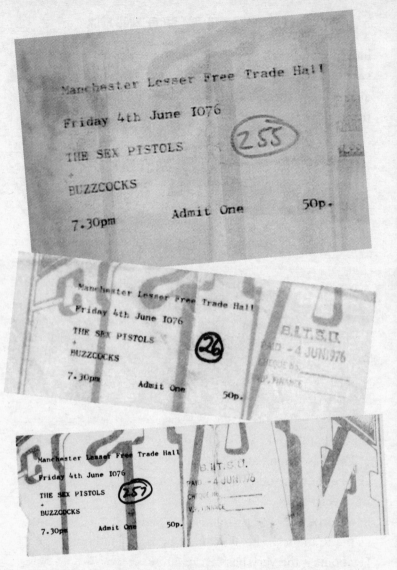

Tickets for the first gig, in all their misprinted glory, belonging to
Peter Oldham, Jon the Postman and Alan Hempsall.

© Peter Oldham, Cathryn Ormrod, Alan Hempsall

CHAPTER TWO

THE THIRD BIGGEST ROCK BAND IN BOLTON

Long of hair, wide of trouser and cheese-clothy of shirt, the suburban youths who took the trouble to make their way to the Lesser Free Trade Hall on 4 June 1976 were about to see the Sex Pistols in their 'punk' prime. That is 'punk' in the old-fashioned sense of the word. Trashy, garage-band punk, 1960s-obsessed and power-chorded.

There is a long-standing and futile argument that has existed for forty-odd years about who 'invented' punk rock. USA versus UK. Put it like this: the British would never have come up with anything as pared down and cartoonish as the Ramones. This green and pleasant land's art-school layabouts – the very basis of its music scene – would have added a whole foundation course of whistles and bells to it. Which is why the closest band Britain has ever produced to 'Da Brudders' – The Damned – have always been snubbed by punk's inner circle since day one. By the same token, the Americans would not and could not have introduced a fully formed attitude and look, attached to the willingness of a nation's youth to adopt it. Which is why it took another fifteen years for the stuff to really catch on in the States. American directness plus British smart stuff equals good punk rock.

The Pistols, in the early summer of 1976, were exactly this. Their choice of cover versions points to a sussed mix of just the right kind of influences. The directness of The Stooges ('No Fun') and the street-smart mod of The Faces ('What'cha Gonna Do About It?'). Rock music un-glammed yet deprived of denim. Sleazy and smart at the same time.

As far as certain sections of the music press were concerned, this was the latest thing, albeit decked out in the second-hand chords and poses of yesteryear. Nonetheless, the name and reputation of the Sex Pistols – aided by Howard and Pete's blossoming promotional skills – had already reached far across the area of northern England that is now known as Greater Manchester.

PETER HOOK: I was living in Little Hulton [the north end of Salford]. I used to read the newspapers quite avidly so I was interested in punk but I just didn't realise what was happening. I remember getting the *Melody Maker* and on the front cover there was a picture of a group fighting at a gig ... and it was the Sex Pistols. I thought, 'My God, this is not the normal thing!' I used to read the *Manchester Evening News* cover to cover all the time and I spotted a little tiny advert for the Lesser Free Trade Hall for the Sex Pistols plus support. It was 50p.

JOHN BERRY (audience member): We liked the idea there was violence at gigs. There was a lot of trouble at gigs at the time and we didn't particularly shy away from that. We quite liked it. We liked that edginess and that atmosphere and that potential for trouble. We came from football backgrounds. So it all fitted with the Sex Pistols. In terms of the Pistols concert, there was myself, Terry Mason, Barney [Bernard Dickin, later Bernard Sumner], Peter Hook and I think both their girlfriends came. And there was another guy called Crazy Mike. Why did we call him that? He had a reputation for jumping off buildings and generally causing murder and mayhem wherever he went.

TERRY MASON (audience member): There wasn't a hierarchy in our gang as such. We were more like a number of federations. It was all based around scooters. Barney had a GP200. That was when the cool skins – suedeheads – had scooters. Then the licensing changed and people ended up with 'fizzies' [50cc mopeds]. We were cool young lads. When you parked your scooter outside the chippy, girls would come up and talk to you. That's the whole point of scooters. We used to go to a nightclub in Salford called The Cattle Market. It was like ... a cattle market; a traditional territorial club. You knew almost everyone in there. You felt safe. But God help anyone from outside.

IAN MOSS: There had been a piece in *New Musical Express* about a gig they played and there was a photographic kind of fracas. There was the famous quote, 'It's not about the music, it's the chaos,' or something. That interested you, because, prior to that, it was all about horrible musician-y things that normal people didn't know about, like scales and beats to a bar.

DAWN BRADBURY (audience member): In 1976 I was sitting my exams at school. I was into music from a very early age – Lou Reed, Iggy Pop, David Bowie, a bit of T. Rex. The first ever gig I went to was Lou Reed And The Velvet Underground featuring Nico. I was twelve. Two weeks later I saw David Bowie and the Spiders From Mars. Aged twelve! I begged my mum and dad to let me go.

JOHN BERRY: We had no idea what the Sex Pistols' music was like but we were avid readers of *Sounds* and *NME* and it sounded right up our street. We liked obnoxious kind of stuff. We thought ... a band that can't play? That'll be great!

JON THE POSTMAN: I'd been buying the *NME* since August 1969, since I was thirteen. I read a review in February 1976, this band the Sex Pistols were playing some small pub in London and it mentioned they were playing a Stooges number, 'No Fun', and that was my favourite Stooges number. So I was very intrigued. When I heard they were playing in Manchester, me and my friends had to go and see them.

PAUL MORLEY: I worked in a bookshop in Stockport [south Manchester], I left school and didn't know what I wanted to do. I worked in this bookshop and it was kind of like my university in a way, it was like an education. I'll always remember that nobody would come in the shop on a Wednesday, so I would just read and read and read. I was really into music and I used to nip into Manchester where I found a shop that sold bootlegs – Dylan and Led Zeppelin bootlegs.

PETER OLDHAM (audience member): I grew up in Denton [east Manchester]. I went to art college doing a photographic course ... but always with an interest in music. Come Thursday, get the *NME*, scour through it, see what was on and go and see bands. We always thought a performance was a lot more valuable than a record. So to go into town [Manchester] and go down to the Free Trade Hall was nice, cheap entertainment. The kind of bands? Camel, Uriah Heep, all the old concept bands ... all very stodgy really, but it was good fun. It was basically all that was on offer, what was about at the time, then punk came along ... that night, as it happens.

PAUL WELSH (audience member – editor *Penetration* magazine): I was a window cleaner and I decided to do a magazine. I was going to see bands like Hawkwind and

Gong. I'd started a magazine previously called *Purple Smoke* – it was more of an arts magazine with stories, poetry, illustrations and recipes. And pictures of nude women. That ran for four issues. Someone told me it was the worst magazine in the world, which I was quite happy about. I decided to do something more professional and about music – I was very influenced by *ZigZag* magazine and Andy Warhol's *Interview* magazine – so that's when I decided to do *Penetration*. It was a good way to hang out with bands and a way to promote the sort of bands I enjoyed listening to. I liked The Stooges and I decided that, whatever the magazine was going to be called, it was going to be named after a Stooges track. 'Search and Destroy' and 'Raw Power' seemed a bit obvious ... and they had this track 'Penetration'. I was thinking in terms of penetrating interviews, not a sexual thing. I read the *NME* article, THE SEX PISTOLS ARE COMING, and read that they did Stooges numbers. So I thought ... I've really got to see them. I'd been to see [Manchester comedy rockers] Alberto y Lost Trios Paranoias and, as I was coming out, someone handed me a flyer for 'Sex Pistols at the Lesser Free Trade Hall'. I got tickets. I was so excited all week. Finally, I was going to see a band that did Stooges numbers and who liked the New York Dolls. I thought, 'I'll review it for the magazine and take some photographs.'

PAUL MORLEY: As soon as certain writers you really favoured started writing in an interesting way about the Sex Pistols, plus their name, plus their look, plus the names of the people in the group ... as soon as you heard there was any chance of them coming up to Manchester, you had to be interested in that.

ALAN HEMPSALL (audience member/musician): Levenshulme, Manchester ... born and bred there. Born in September 1960. I was still living at home at the time in question, 4 Jun 1976. I was fifteen years old. I think Levenshulme had an ambience of being slightly better off than north Manchester, it wasn't pure *Coronation Street*, there were little gardens in the front. Obviously *Sounds* and *NME* were a must. I used to buy *Sounds* strangely more than *NME*, but obviously it varied depending on who was on the front cover. I went to school in Gorton and you had a choice of glam rock ... and everybody was into Bowie or Alice Cooper ... or if you wanted to get a bit more cerebral, you got into Led Zeppelin or you got into Emerson Lake & Palmer.

TONY WILSON: Was Alan at it? Fucking hell...

Meanwhile, the Pistols were heading north, expecting to get full musical support from the promised Devoto/Shelley band. Thanks to their poor performance at their debut gig in Bolton on 1 April, they felt that they just weren't quite ready. So, although the fact that the tickets had already been made and quite clearly stated that the gig would feature the 'Sex Pistols + Buzzcocks', a replacement band had to be found. Sharpish. Howard and Pete's reputation

47

as promoters was on the line here and there was no way they could charge 50p to see just one band, even if that band was the Sex Pistols.

HOWARD DEVOTO: Because we weren't ready, we needed to draft somebody else in to play support. We didn't know anybody. The only thing I could remember was this guy – I think his name was Geoff – that I worked with the previous summer at a mail-order warehouse in Manchester doing a holiday job as a student. This guy was in a band.

PETE SHELLEY: There was a band called the Mandela Band or Mandala Band. Don't know which one it was. They were a bit 'hippy trippy' type thing. I never saw them though because I was collecting the tickets.

HOWARD DEVOTO: It wasn't the Mandala Band. It was a group called Solstice, not the Mandala band. They did things like 'Nantucket Sleighride' which is, I think, a tune by Mountain. I just remember Geoff in this white boiler suit...

PETE SHELLEY: It could have been Solstice. It could have been. I think Howard would probably know because he conspired with them ... but we never played with them again after that.

Geoff Wild was the leader of Solstice, one of the three biggest bands based in Bolton at the time. The other big groups were called Legend and Iron Maiden. Not that Iron Maiden – the other lot, from Bolton. Along with Geoff on guitar, Solstice were 'Kimble' on vocals, Paul Flintoff on bass, Harry Box on drums and Dave 'Zok' Howard on keyboards. With Neal Holden on lights and Dave Eyre on sound, they operated as a collective, splitting the money seven ways. For decades, no one managed to trace Solstice. As a result, they were denied their place in the footnotes of rock history.

DAVE EYRE (soundman – Solstice): Geoff used to work at the Beehive Mill in Bolton with Howard Devoto, labouring. Howard got this gig lined up with the Sex Pistols at the Lesser Free Trade Hall but, for some reason, they weren't ready. They asked if we'd do it ... at the time we'd do anything.

DAVE HOWARD (keyboard player – Solstice): We used to play at The Phoenix in Manchester, the Mardi Gras in Blackpool – which was a gay club – The Town Hall pub in Eccles and the Bolton Institute, where Howard Devoto may have seen us.

NEAL HOLDEN (lighting – Solstice): Anytime there was a gig, we were the sharpest. The most professional. We had a travelling fanbase of three or four hundred people who'd follow us around. We always did a professional show. We had lights. We had a smoke machine.

DAVE HOWARD: We used to do stuff like 'Nantucket Sleighride', which went down well. A lot of Santana stuff, Deep Purple stuff, Rory Gallagher, Steve Miller, Uriah Heep, the Welsh band, Man. Typical rock-standard stuff. Plus a few originals.

DAVE EYRE: There was one Zok wrote called 'Amnesia' – that used to go down a storm, it was really good.

DAVE HOWARD: It was a pile of shite.

So, despite what the tickets said, Sex Pistols were not supported by Buzzcocks. They were supported by Howard's workmate Geoff and his group Solstice. The third biggest rock band in Bolton.

DAWN BRADBURY: My best friend at school was a girl called Carol McQueeney who went out with a guy called Harry Box, an amateur drummer in Solstice. They were easy listening, middle-of-the road rock and they got this gig at the Lesser Free Trade Hall. The day of the Pistols' gig I took my English Literature O Level – it had just been my birthday so I was sixteen years and ten days old. Hence my claim to being the youngest ever punk in Manchester.

TONY WILSON: Why did I go? Maybe there was this feeling, there was an appetite ... Oh my God, there's something new. I mean, now, I walk around the world, desperate and waiting and I go and see anything, because it might be the new thing. Good God ... I'd even go to Leeds. Anyway, I go ... it was in the diary, 4 June.

HOWARD DEVOTO: On the night of the first gig, I was probably running around the hall, doing all the kinds of things you do ... trying to make sure it all happens. I'd just bought the first Ramones album on import – and I discovered the house PA system – so, I was doing the interval music.

TONY WILSON: I had no knowledge of the Ramones. I had no backwards knowledge, as the Stretford schoolboy Morrissey had, of the New York Dolls. And I wasn't even really aware of Iggy Pop.

PETE SHELLEY: I was in the box office selling tickets and Malcolm McLaren was coming down to see how many people were wandering around outside, there was a chalk board ... big letters, 'LIVE FROM LONDON – THE SEX PISTOLS', he was saying things to people like, 'Oh, there's this band from London ... the Sex Pistols, they're great, they're fantastic, they're really famous.' So it was all a big game ... it was a big con trick. It was all a big con trick to get people to part with 50p.

One of those who fell for this was Steve Diggle. He would never have ended up in Buzzcocks if he hadn't gone along by mistake, thinking he was auditioning for a band, only to be seduced by Malcolm's spiel.

STEVE DIGGLE: I answered an ad in the *Manchester Evening News*. My dad had nicked me a bass off the back of this truck. I had a guitar and I wanted to be a guitarist, but I thought there are always ads for bass players and drummers. I answered this ad and I spoke to this guy and I said, 'Let's meet at the Free Trade Hall,' because there was a pub called Cox's Bar round the corner. I was stood outside waiting for this guy when I met Malcolm McLaren and he said, 'They're inside.'

PETE SHELLEY: We didn't have a bass player or a drummer. Howard had a phone call that afternoon on 4 June, from somebody who left a message, saying they were a bass player and Malcolm McLaren overheard this. Later, he'd gone outside, got talking to a bloke ... 'Sex Pistols, inside, do you want to come and see them?' This bloke says, 'No, I'm waiting to meet someone.' Malcolm said, 'Are you the bass player?' He said, 'Yes'. 'Oh, they're inside.' He came in and said, 'Here's your new bass player,' and I met Steve Diggle.

STEVE DIGGLE: Pete Shelley's collecting tickets on the door, you know. He and Howard had put an ad in the *Manchester Review*, looking for a bass player and a drummer and they thought it was me. We were talking at cross-purposes for about twenty minutes.

PETE SHELLEY: He was actually waiting to meet a completely different bloke, because about five minutes later,

Malcolm came in with somebody else saying, 'It's your guitarist.' Never saw him again. I went up and I started talking to Steve and he'd just discovered the error of his ways. He'd actually replied to another advert for a lead guitarist but ended up with me instead. So I said, 'Right, well, while you're here, why don't you see the band? We're trying to do stuff like that.' So he liked it and we arranged that he would come over to Howard's rehearsal place the next day. He was a bass player and he had a bass guitar: it was perfect – it was like he fell out of the sky.

Devoto and Shelley were the only ones at the Lesser Free Trade Hall who had actually seen the Pistols play live before. For everyone else, there were few expectations other than the promise of an unusual name.

MALCOLM MCLAREN: You were never looking to hopefully see a good rock 'n' roll band, you were looking and hoping to see the most dreadful and wonderful energy ... that could be best described as your first fuck, really.

NEAL HOLDEN: I knew it was going to be a strange gig because I got in the lift with Malcolm McLaren and he had this leather Stetson on. And a full leather outfit. I thought, definitely a very odd person.

PAUL WELSH: I saw Malcolm McLaren and gave him a copy of *Penetration*. I remember him wearing a fur coat

– he was standing at the back with a smirk on his face, like he was a dad at a school pantomime watching his kids perform. He had a satisfied smile.

DAVE EYRE: We didn't know the Sex Pistols from Adam. We had a very small, basic PA system. They brought in the works. I'm setting our PA up and Johnny Rotten comes up to me and says [adopts Cockney whine], 'D'you wanna hire our PA?' I said, 'How much?' and he , 'Fifty quid.' 'Err, no thanks, we'll manage.' We weren't even getting fifty quid for the gig.

NEAL HOLDEN: That upset us. Normal practice was for the main band to let the support use the PA. They tried to rip us off for money. Somebody pinched our singer's guitar strap and he had to threaten them to get it back. It wasn't a friendly gig. We did our job as professionally as possible.

JOHN BERRY: It was up some stairs. I remember Malcolm McLaren dressed in a leather outfit. The only people we knew that wore leather were Hell's Angels. There weren't a lot of guys in Manchester that looked like that. We went in and it was small. Very small. We kind of slunk at the back and kept our heads down just in case.

IAIN GREY (audience member): When we got there, on the door there's this guy who totally freaked me out. One-piece leather outfit, a space-age teddy boy. He was Malcolm McLaren and he just looked so cool. He was saying to us, 'Oh, don't come in yet, the support band are on at the moment and they're crap. Come back in half an hour.' I felt old and he was, like, ten years older than me. But he was so cool.

EDDIE GARRITY: Yeah, well, Iain Grey, he used to be a devotee of *NME*. He'd read that this new thing was happening 'cause I wasn't really into it at all, that sort of caper. And he said, 'There's something really going to be big happening in Manchester and we've got to be there,' so I went along with him really.

PETER HOOK: The way they were dressed was absolutely bizarre, Malcolm McLaren dressed in leather in the ticket booth, giving out tickets as you walked in. Then he came and sat at the end of our row. I'd never seen anybody bloody dressed in leather, I'd seen Alvin Stardust on telly, but I'd never seen anything like that in my life.

TONY WILSON: My memories were, Malcolm wearing black leather trousers and a black leather jacket. Years later, I discovered that this whole thing had been to sell leather trousers.

ALAN HEMPSALL: We arrived in good time and just scurried straight to the front. It was a seated auditorium.

DAWN BRADBURY: I didn't pay to get in – I was on the guest list because Harry was playing with Solstice. That boosted the numbers, the fact that Solstice had eight or nine people on the guest list. The top of the bill? I'd heard there was some new London band coming up. Solstice were on the bill to drag the hippies in – I don't think the Pistols would have had much of an audience had it not been for Solstice, which is a bit bizarre.

IAN MOSS: I ended up going on my own. I phoned various girls up to see if they wanted to go, but just the name 'Sex Pistols' seemed to put them off.

JORDAN: It was very weird because you never knew what was going to happen, you'd turn up somewhere and people didn't know who the Sex Pistols were, they'd just come in to see a gig. You'd get a bad reception and you knew it was very groundbreaking. People were amazed and blinkin' blown away by it. However, a lot of people travelled. A lot of fans travelled to see every gig. It's almost like they knew it was going to be ... *history*. We got a load of fans that were really very well known.

TONY WILSON: All I knew it was ... the Lesser Free Trade Hall and this band the Sex Pistols. I didn't know the Buzzcocks were meant to play or anything. I didn't even know the Buzzcocks did or didn't exist at that point in my life. I knew that Howard Trafford/Devoto had sent me the tape. The person I actually talked to at the gig was the geezer in black leather trousers and the black leather jacket, which was Mr McLaren, who said hello to me and I said hello to him.

PETE SHELLEY: I knew of him [Wilson] because I used to watch him on TV every night. I don't know ... I've no strong recollection of him being at the first one. I don't actually remember him coming up to the box office saying, 'I'm on the guest list,' or anything like that. It would fit more that he would be at the second one rather than the first.

HOWARD DEVOTO: Whether he [Wilson] actually came to that one, I don't know. I don't think he'd make it up. I think whatever he says is probably the truth.

TONY WILSON: It's confusing as to who was there. Certainly Morrissey was there. Steven was the little writer kid; the 'little intellectual at the back'. He was a friend of McLaren's 'cause of his fondness of the New York Dolls. This is Steven Morrissey, probably aged about fifteen. I'm pretty sure Hucknall [Mick – Simply Red] was there. I think at least two members of Joy Division were there. I think Mark E. Smith [The Fall] was there.

IAN MOSS: Mick Hucknall wasn't at the Lesser Free Trade Hall. I should know, my brother Neil was in [Hucknall's first band] The Frantic Elevators.

ALAN HEMPSALL: I would say thirty to fifty people, tops, were there. The only person that I can say for sure was there is Tony Wilson, because I actually spoke to him. I spoke to him because I'd met him at KISS the month before at the Free Trade Hall, the big hall downstairs they'd played in May.

TONY WILSON: I think, when things happen, everyone claims to have been there, so I mean, normal activity really. If some guy says he saw me there and we talked about the KISS gig, that's probably very correct actually. Because we [Granada TV] had just done the KISS concert about two months earlier, a hysterical concert that was in the main auditorium. I presume a lot of people who went to the second Sex Pistols' gig claim to have been at the first gig. I think that's where it gets confused. I mean we now say thirty or forty, could have been more like twenty. It was absolutely empty. I was on holiday for the second gig.

STEVE DIGGLE: They say all these people were there. I don't remember any of them being there. But then I wouldn't have known Morrissey from fucking Adam. I never saw Wilson either – but I was short-sighted in those days...

HOWARD DEVOTO: The only people, apart from Pete Shelley, myself, Steve Diggle and all the Pistols crew that I'd be reasonably certain were there were Paul Morley and Morrissey.

PAUL WELSH: As far as I'm concerned, Paul Morley

wasn't at the first one. He was a friend of ours and, every time I went in his shop to leave copies of the magazine, he'd ask if he could write something for *Penetration*. He was at the KISS concert a few weeks before but I didn't see him at the first Pistols gig. He was the sort of person who would have come over. There was six or seven of us and we all knew him. As far as I'm concerned, he wasn't there. Unless he was hiding at the back somewhere.

HOWARD DEVOTO: Morrissey wrote a letter to the *NME* about the gig...

I pen this epistle after witnessing the infamous Sex Pistols 'in concert' at the Manchester Lesser Free Trade Hall. The bumptious Pistols in jumble sale attire had those few that attended dancing in the aisles despite their discordant music and barely audible audacious lyrics, and they were called back for two encores. The Pistols boast of having no inspiration from the New York/Manhattan scene, yet their set includes 'I'm Not Your Stepping Stone' a number believed to have been done to perfection by the Heartbreakers on any sleazy New York night. The Pistols' vocalist/exhibitionist Johnny Rotten's self-assured 'love us or leave us' approach can be compared to Iggy Pop and David Johanson in their heyday. I'd love to see the Pistols make it. Maybe they'll be able to afford some clothes which don't look as though they've been slept in.

Steve Morrissey, *NME* letters page 27 June, 1976.

HOWARD DEVOTO: Oh, and Jon the Postman.

JON THE POSTMAN: The only people I knew there were my immediate friends I went with. I'm sure Tony Wilson wasn't there. I'd seen him a year before at an Emmylou Harris concert, at the Free Trade Hall, so that's how punky Tony was.

TONY WILSON: Doesn't matter who was there ... just the fact there was *enough* people there.

JON THE POSTMAN: It's hard to say, I mean, I'm not too sure how many people the venue actually holds but I would say probably, between fifty and perhaps eighty people, I would imagine, perhaps a hundred were there.

HOWARD DEVOTO: I think the Lesser Free Trade Hall held about four hundred. We had made the tickets; we had actually hand-crafted those tickets and numbered them. So I think that figure of a hundred is probably as accurate as anybody could come up with. It did not feel full – there's no way around that – and it was seated. And up until right at the end, people stayed seated.

As the audience took their seats, there was disappointment in some areas that the tantalisingly named Buzzcocks were a no-show. But the band that was actually providing warm-up for the main attraction was going down pretty well: Howard's holiday-job friend Geoff and his prog-rockers Solstice.

PETER OLDHAM: We thought, 'Right, yeah, we'll have some of that'. So we went down into this little church-hall type set-up, no stage lighting ... just a little concept band on.

ALAN HEMPSALL: It was weird because there was a band on. The tickets quite clearly said 'Buzzcocks'. Anyway, this band came on stage and, as rock bands like to have in the 1970s, they had their name on the bass drum and it was Solstice. They performed a set of probably around thirty to forty minutes of their own stuff, with one or two rock standards. My abiding memory of the support group is that the singer had a droopy moustache but he was also sporting a love bite on his neck. They did this absolutely faithful version of 'Nantucket Sleighride'. It was the theme tune of the political television programme which you might remember called *Weekend World*.

GLEN MATLOCK: Right, well, I like Mountain ... See, the thing is, I was more than likely in Tommy Ducks when they was on...

Tommy Ducks was a popular and somewhat racy Manchester pub, several hundred yards from the Free Trade Hall on East Street. The pub had a glass-covered coffin as a table and fornicating ducks printed on its glasses. Its main selling point though was its collection of female customers' recently removed knickers. On their first visit to the pub, women were invited to remove their underwear to add to the collection. A group of feminists once stormed the pub and tried to – if you will – pull the knickers down.

PETE SHELLEY: We always used to take the Sex Pistols to Tommy Ducks. They liked Tommy Ducks because they stuck ladies' underwear up on the ceiling and they thought that was amazing. So every time they came they said, 'Let's go to Tommy Ducks!'

JORDAN: I remember Pete Shelley taking me to Tommy Ducks, where there's all these knickers on the ceiling. There's no other time I would have been taken there, so I guess I must have been there. Yeah ... I swear I was there!

HOWARD DEVOTO: I don't recall seeing anybody in the hall that I thought, 'There's a punk.' Pete and I had changed our look considerably and got very curious looks from the Teds in Piccadilly [Manchester's central gardens area]. I don't really recall anybody at that gig looking like a punk – a mostly male audience looking like Manchester males did in those days.

EDDIE GARRITY: Well, I remember there wasn't really a lot of people there. You know, there was a lot of hype about it in the paper. We got there expecting to see a massive crowd, you know, and there were no queues or anything and some really scruffy git on the door. It was 50p or something daft and you'd just go upstairs into this empty hall.

PETER HOOK: Solstice were old, complete dyed-in-the-wool, Deep Purple/Led Zeppelin-type rockers. I remember there were very, very few people there. About forty or something.

PAUL MORLEY: Solstice played a load of cover versions of songs by the Allman Brothers or Mountain or Man. There was this fantastic Welsh group called Man who were like the British Grateful Dead and they had an album called *Be Good To Yourself At Least Once A Day*, that came with a free fold-up map of Wales. They did this song called 'Bananas' ... 'I like to eat bananas because they've got no bones ... I like marijuana because it gets me stoned.' Being a Man fan, I was aware that this group was doing it and I thought this was pretty good. Fantastic, how great is that?

HOWARD DEVOTO: I think Solstice had a strobe light, one of those you'd have seen in your local pub. You'd have thought they were pretty good, actually. But they were not the right vibe at all really. But what the hell. A few people clapped. They weren't booed off or anything like that.

JOHN BERRY: We sat through Solstice – we'd never heard of them. We had no idea Buzzcocks were supposed to play. I think it's on the ticket. It was a very muted atmosphere. In our little group there was a sense of ... 'Something's going to happen.' Maybe we *wanted* something to happen.

PAUL MORLEY: The first Sex Pistols show, I went on my own, and my memory of it really is that everyone was just sort of very polite ... and the fact that we were seated. And there wasn't many people there. The smallness of the venue and the fact it was seated made it feel a little bit like something you might come across in your school, like some kind of weird assembly or something. I wrote about it instantly for a fanzine I was doing and I've described everybody being there like furry freaks or plastic posers. I still had long hair and I believe some form of facial hair. I think I just got the feeling that everybody watched it with a kind of strange trepidation. We just didn't know what the heck was about to happen and that was further encouraged by the fact that the support group were a bunch of furry freaks. They were a bunch of heavy metal kind of guys in flared denim, the whole thing that obviously was being wrenched away by the Sex Pistols.

IAN MOSS: The support band worried me. They were just another typical rock band playing rock music. I thought, 'Have I wasted a Friday night here? Are the Sex Pistols just going to be another version of this?' That was what people were used to seeing – it was disappointing. They probably got a nice round of applause for their efforts. It certainly wasn't memorable.

JON THE POSTMAN: Well, I went with quite a few friends, I think there were about eight of us went and we saw this support band, and they were like dreadful, they were like the arse-end of prog rock. They were tolerated.

PAUL WELSH: I saw the first few minutes and went back to the bar. It wasn't what I was expecting. We just wanted the Sex Pistols to come on.

PETER OLDHAM: Very polite applause at first and then they came on with 'Nantucket Sleighride'. Everybody was quite keen on that one. They shovelled off and then the main act came on.

PAUL MORLEY: Of course, they were the most inappropriate group to have, but, in another sense they lulled us into a false sense of security and made what was about to happen even more dramatic.

DAVE HOWARD: It was a very laid-back audience. We went down OK. Not fantastic.

PETER OLDHAM: It was more a matter of everybody turning up in cheesecloth and flared trousers ... there was no such thing as punk in Manchester. I suppose you could say Slaughter And The Dogs were at it somewhere.

HOWARD DEVOTO: Longish hair, I don't know, duffel coats. Paul Morley always looked like Francis Rossi out of

Status Quo to me, with his long hair. The audience would have all looked like Solstice fans.

PAUL MORLEY: Unfortunately, he's very, very accurate. You know, I didn't even get my hair cut for the second Sex Pistols gig. The next time they played, Johnny Rotten wouldn't talk to me. He actually said, 'I ain't talking to you, you look like a student.' That was the moment I got my hair cut. I went home and cut it with blunt scissors and ended up looking probably more like Rod Stewart. But at the time at least it took me away from the Francis Rossi area.

IAN MOSS: I've a horrible feeling that I was wearing a beige suit.

JON THE POSTMAN: People didn't know what a punk-rock gig was. That was the first time the Pistols had been in Manchester.

TONY WILSON: There was this old-fashioned little theatre, with a very high proscenium stage and about thirty or forty of us, sitting separately in these seats. I was on my own. We all sat there and ... my prime memory is of me being like that [pulls startled face] and I think everyone else was just like that [pulls startled face again] ... shocked.

DAVE HOWARD: We'd played and we'd gone down all right. Then this lot came on and they were bloody crap. Me and Geoff pissed off to the pub round the corner.

SEX PISTOLS

Rotten vocalist of the year No.1 * * *

Well, at last our prayers have been answered with the 'Sex Pistols'. They are musically everything that a Velvet Underground, Stooges, New York Dolls freak could wish for, while visually they look like poor customers at a jumble sale, tacky, sleazy, distasteful and yet somewhat natural.

They attack their numbers as if they were attacking a gang of thugs in a street fight, viciously. "We hate everything" they emphasise in their press kit; and that means you!

They hail from Shepherds Bush and Finsbury Park and met at 'Sex' the shop, in Chelsea's World's End, owned by Malcolm McLaren. McLaren encouraged the boys to form 'Sex Pistols'; Johnny Rotten, vocals; Steve Jones on guitar; Glen Matlock pumping bass chords; and Paul Cook, drums. They played the clubs and colleges, gaining unpopularity wherever they went, ultimately ending in a ban at the Marquee.

McLaren created a regular venue for them at the 'El Paradise' strip club in Soho, a perfect setting. Instead of stripping clothes, they stripped music to the bare minimum of finesse.

Included in their repertoire is 'Substitute' by the Who, 'No Fun', the Stooges, 'Looking for a Kiss', the New York Dolls and 'What You Gonna Do About It', the Small Faces. As well as the aforementioned classics, they do their own originals 'Pretty Vacant', 'Submission', 'Only Seventeen', 'Problems', 'No Feelings' and 'I'm a Lazy Pseud', among others.

They were sacked as 'Eddie and the Hotrods' support act for, as 'Eddie and the Hotrods explained, "kicking their monitors about". What rotters. The N.M.E. once suggested that the 'Pistols' use 'plants' as hecklers in the audience, but my rubber plant hasn't ever been known to heckle anyone. 'Sounds' suggest that they are the Stones of the late seventies. 'The Sex Pistols' would, however, blow the Stones off-stage anyday. The past must concede to the facts. "They do as much for music as World War Two did for the cause of peace" was Melody Makers' theory.

"I hate shit" is Johnny Rotten's explanation. "I want to change it so there are rock bands like us."

They blitz the audience with power chords and vocals set in a different key to the music. When I saw them, they whipped the audience to a frenzy with ease and, when responded to, Johnny Rotten actually smiled!

'Sex Pistols' are, at the moment, unique and they're amazing live, but I'll leave you to form your own opinions, see them soon.

Band of the year No.1

'Vocals and power chords set in a completely different key to the music': The only ever review of the Pistols' first gig at the Lesser Free Trade Hall, from *Penetration Magazine.© Paul Welsh*

CHAPTER THREE

INTIMIDATION ON LEGS

If there's a moment that would forever symbolise the change that was about to hit British music, it can be highlighted as being the gap between Solstice leaving the stage of the Lesser Free Trade Hall and the Sex Pistols walking onto it. Because The Gig That Changed The World is about to get underway.

DAWN BRADBURY: Solstice played. All nice. Then the Pistols came on. I didn't know what to expect, other than I'd heard they were completely different to anything I'd ever heard before ... but you get that a lot. You think yeah, yeah, of course. Then out they came ... and they *were* completely different. It blew my mind.

Despite their reputation as doyens of the King's Road and dedicated followers of fashion ... the Pistols are dressed appallingly. Rotten is wearing a ripped yellow jumper and T-shirt along with a pair of old bloke's Oxfam trousers. Jones is in an all-in-one boiler suit. Matlock sports a plain T-shirt and a pair of Jackson Pollock paint-splattered trousers. Not much Chelsea couture on show here. At the back of the hall a hand-held camera whirrs into life, capturing the Pistols on Super 8mm; Mark Roberts, a student pal of Howard's, has brought his camera.

Somewhere else in the room another audience member reaches down to their leg, where a tape machine has been strapped, and presses record. This tape will form the basis of a bootleg LP that will be made to mark the gig. The only other record of the event is a set of photographs by Paul Welsh, the man behind the seminal Manchester fanzine *Penetration*. Thanks to Paul, we can actually see the gig that changed the world and the audience. Welsh was a proto-punk glam rocker who wore leather trousers and women's jewellery and covered his face in talcum powder to make himself look ill, earning himself the nickname 'Pasty Paul'.

PAUL WELSH: The people I was with – I went with Jon the Postman – all said they wanted a set of pictures of the Pistols. When we were in the bar, the band came in. My friends said, 'Forget it, we don't want pictures of those ugly bastards.' By the end of the gig, they'd changed their minds again. They *really did* want pictures.

IAIN GREY: Johnny Rotten ambled on ... and that was like just a shock. He was one of the most frightening people

I'd ever seen at that time ... this lad with a thousand-yard stare, just stood there. And then they started playing ... and it was as though he was just staring at me. He was probably just looking out to the audience.

PAUL MORLEY: He meant it, maaaan ... and you felt that more than anything you'd ever come across before. That he was really living it out and that, at the time, was quite unusual and completely refreshing. We've lost it again now, so it still seems to have a real kind of potency, even though it was rock music, it was absolutely expressing something deep and important to himself and you kind of got that, rather than any individual sense of the songs.

JON THE POSTMAN: Of course, when the Pistols came on stage that was a revelation – it was like the first time I'd ever seen our contemporaries playing the sort of music that we were into.

ALAN HEMPSALL: The Sex Pistols came on and they looked as you remember them from loads of press photographs. John Rotten had a T-shirt with the word 'TITS' emblazoned in sequins. They had these thick brothel creepers on. My friend who's sat right next to me, he's a bit of a wag. He shouts out, 'You're not very sexy are you?' Lydon just shot him this look and sneered, 'Why, do you want some sex?'

JOHN BERRY: With hindsight, it was an act – the goading of the audience – because it wasn't an antagonistic crowd. It was a Mancunian audience. We didn't fucking care one way or the other.

IAN MOSS: I think the audience was sat there waiting to be impressed ... or disappointed. So the attitude was coming from the stage and almost exclusively from Johnny Rotten ... just the way he moved, the way he sounded, the little asides between songs. It was just not like some preening rock star, it was a completely different performance to any I'd ever seen and I'd seen hundreds of bands. Completely different.

PAUL MORLEY: You could stare into the whites of his eyes. It was terrifying and addictive. It was fantastic. The Sex Pistols coming to Manchester is interesting because they didn't go to Liverpool and they didn't go to Glasgow or Sheffield.

STEVE DIGGLE: Me and Pete Shelley kind of sat at the back discussing what we were going to do and on came the Sex Pistols. To me, it was like the birth of Christ – Bethlehem! – that's how great they were. I'd say that was where punk rock was born, that night – far more so than London.

PETER OLDHAM: They played 'Pretty Vacant'. It was intimidation on legs. These guys came out and BANG! It was there.

TONY WILSON: Then you begin to understand what they were doing ... just playing ridiculously fast, and just putting loads of energy into it. Just doing it ... and doing it properly. It was absolutely real ... everything else was unreal. It's been five, six, seven years since one had encountered anything real – on stage, in music. It was real, it was ... heaven knows what it was, it was just, Oh God ... I've been waiting for this. God, it's real.

JOHN BERRY: The noise was tremendous. We'd been to a lot of loud concerts – we'd seen The Who at Belle Vue – but this was *fucking noisy*. We knew none of the tunes. We could just about make out 'Substitute'. We wouldn't have known songs like 'Steppin' Stone'. I don't think any of us had heard any of their music up until that point. But this was a racket. It was a cacophony of sound. We hadn't seen anything like it.

DAVE HOWARD: The Pistols came on and it was so loud. To be honest, I didn't like it. I know it's iconic now, but then it was so new and different to what we were doing. Every song ended with, 'Why don't you all fuck off?'

PAUL WELSH: It was discordant and not very professional. It was different from the music we'd been listening to.

PAUL MORLEY: You kind of thought, 'Oh, this is interesting, there's thirty or forty other people that are clearly interested in newness'. You just kind of half-acknowledged that there were other kinds of strange people interested in this new music but you had no idea who they were. There was nobody I'd even recognise. They just popped out fresh, so you just get this vague feeling of people milling about in a slightly transfixed sense.

DAWN BRADBURY: I think I was in shock for the first three numbers. It took a little while, it's not like I was hooked in the first minute of the first track. It took a few numbers for me to feel it. They weren't on for that long. It was about halfway though ... Then I was hooked for life.

PAUL WELSH: There were only people in the first four or five rows. The rest of the place was empty. That made it different from concerts we were used to. You'd go into the main Free Trade Hall and it would be packed. But you knew that the people at the Pistols gig were like-minded. They'd read about them.

DAVE EYRE: Me and Paul, the bass player, went exploring. We climbed down onto the stage of the main Free Trade Hall below while the Pistols were playing. Standing on this big stage thinking, 'Wouldn't it be great to play here...'

A bootleg recording of the gig reveals that the Pistols played 'Don't Gimme Me No Lip Child', 'I Did You No Wrong', 'Substitute', 'No Feelings', 'Steppin' Stone' and

'Pretty Vacant'. 'Submission' is introduced as 'a pop song.' There is a great deal of shouting from the audience. 'Get off! You're crap!' one audience member cries. 'Got a lot of mouth, sat there in the dark,' Rotten declares. 'If you don't like it, fuck off out of it,' he says, before the band launch into 'What'cha Gonna Do About It?' by the Small Faces. Glen Matlock can be heard, quite clearly, doing harmonies to accompany Rotten's lead vocal. They play 'No Fun' twice after failing to agree with the crowd on what they should do by way of an encore. Rotten even offers to play some Osmonds. 'This is dying a death,' he says from the stage. If, as many people have stated, there are only a few dozen there, then they are a very noisy few dozen indeed. Towards the end, with people clearly out of their seats, Rotten wonders out loud where everyone has come from.

IAN MOSS: Quite late into the gig, there was a bit of banter from the audience to the stage. They were shouting out the names of bands. You know, 'The 13th Floor Elevators! What do you think of them?' Then somebody shouted, 'Eddie And The Hot Rods!' and Rotten looked and he said, 'Our imitators...'

JON THE POSTMAN: That was me and my friends. We were shouting out, 'The Stooges,' and, 'MC5,' and one of my friends was shouting out, 'Eddie And The Hot Rods,' and Lydon hated Eddie And The Hot Rods ... so, of course, we heckled them further.

JOHN BERRY: There was a bit of head nodding. I don't recall much clapping. I think one guy got up to dance. It may have been Jon the Postman.

PAUL MORLEY: It was erotically charged, the whole thing was erotic. You know, the funny thing is they could play really well. Amongst the more 'pseud' of us, that was something that was important. It wasn't a shambles at all, they were very powerful and they had all the right moves. I just remember at that first show, really being in a kind of state of shock almost. I was quite still, absorbing it all. A kind of remarkable revolution had happened, within a music that still used guitars and covered The Who and the Small Faces, it still had the obvious reference points. It was still rock 'n' roll, it was very much about that ... but plus all the sexiness you wanted from the music and the anger and the power. It just seemed to be condensed into it and I was just transfixed.

PETER HOOK: The band played really well, but the sound was terrible. Johnny Rotten had his own unique style of singing ... everybody thought they were rubbish – that was down to the sound guy, it's really the sound guy that's responsible for me thinking I could form a band. If you listen to the bootleg, they're actually playing quite well. I mean they were quite an established rhythm section, Paul Cook and Matlock. Steve Jones could actually play guitar. It was so aggressive and it was that that actually turned you on.

TONY WILSON: Steve Jones was wearing a boiler suit and his entire act was a Pete Townshend impersonation.

IAN MOSS: Johnny Rotten had this kind of ratty pullover on, you could see the cigarette burns on his arm. A lot of people in hindsight say to me, 'What we liked about them was they were rubbish.' But they didn't sound rubbish to me, they sounded magnificent. They patently could play. It was rudimentary, but it was tight.

JON THE POSTMAN: Yeah, it was very powerful and raw and immediate and everything that we'd hoped for from a band ... our contemporaries live on stage. They certainly looked different. They had short hair for a kick-off which was not the norm at the time at all. Most people had the long style of hair of ... you know ... the straights. So it was definitely different.

GLEN MATLOCK: We were supposed to have short hair and it's a surprise quite how long our hair was. It does look quite tame in comparison to what punks were supposed to look like.

TONY WILSON: They did 'Steppin' Stone' by The Monkees and suddenly you go, 'Oh, wow ... I get it ... fine.' But it was basically sitting with your mouth open thinking, 'Good Heavens'. It happened again for me, thirteen years later in The Haçienda. The first time it happened, the first time you see rock 'n' roll die ... and then be reborn, you just think, 'Oh my God, what is this?' The next time round it's like, 'Aah ... been here before, isn't this wonderful?' At the time I think I had my mouth open. I was probably swallowing fucking flies.

PAUL MORLEY: The kind of rock music that you'd loved over the years, like Led Zeppelin, The Who and The Rolling Stones, that seemed a little bit before your time. The Pistols brought everything bang up to date, it was absolutely for you. It was about the times. You couldn't really get any idea what they were singing about, but you just had a gut instinct that this was about how you felt. And about the nation. And about how pissed off you were. And about what you were expected to accept as a teenager. And about how fucked up your future was going to be. You just knew that's what it was all about, even with the mayhem that was being caused. It was nothing to do with pop music in that sense – it was much more than that. It was a big bizarre philosophy being thrown at you and that was incredibly exciting.

PETE SHELLEY: They were excellent. They made all the hairs on the back of your neck stand up.

EDDIE GARRITY: Well, they were just dreadful ... that first gig, totally unrehearsed. I think they'd just gone out of their way to just get noticed and be as bad as they possibly could be.

TONY WILSON: Most of pop music – and most of rock 'n' roll – is not real. The guys are just people, just playing guitars or singing because they're good at it and it sounds good. That isn't rock 'n' roll. That isn't pop music. Pop music and rock 'n' roll is when someone means it, that's when it's real. For me, personally, academically, it wasn't until about the seventh number ... they did all these other numbers and the seventh number was 'Steppin' Stone'. You can imagine Johnny singing and suddenly there's a song that you knew, being done by this bunch of maniacs.

HOWARD DEVOTO: It wasn't chaotic or anything like that. Prior to the gig, the Sex Pistols had gone out for a drink with one of my philosophy lecturers, a wonderful man by the name of Mr David Melling. Nice gentleman, of great bearing and dignity. They all went out for a drink in the pub over the road. It's one of those events in one's life ... I would really liked to have been there. They all got on very well and David assured me that they were very nice lads. It's just one of those things where two parts of your life come together and you think, 'My goodness me, there's an existential happening!'

PETER OLDHAM: It was more like the audience reaction in *The Producers* [film featuring the song 'Springtime for Hitler']. The audience was sat there with their mouths open. After they finished, they weren't quite sure whether they were good or what. But the attack and the aggression of it was something to behold.

JOHN BERRY: I don't think a lot of us were that impressed. We had no knowledge of the *avant garde* – we were naive kids from Salford. But I liked the image I saw on stage. It was shocking. It was an image and a half. And it was a noise and a half.

MALCOLM MCLAREN: I can only remember that those kids were believing that they were at the beginning of something. And they believed they had in their reach something authentic. And they were not going to ever let that go. A rare jewel ... like a ruby in a field of tin.

GLEN MATLOCK: ...So I'm told. And I know people who were at the gig. But I mean, when you're in a band you kind of get taken to where you're going ... and what happens when you get there is not totally within your hands.

TERRY MASON: They seemed to be getting on with it and having a good time. We thought, 'Why can't we have a go?'

JOHN BERRY: When it ended, quite a few people went to the front to have a chat with Johnny Rotten. He was very friendly! He'd stopped his act. He was now the guy from London who wanted to spread the word. When it had finished and we drifted off, there were varying opinions about what had happened. The girls in the group were not enamoured with the noise. Crazy Mike wasn't enamoured with it either. I think the rest of us were quite shocked. We probably went to Cox's bar round the back for a few more pints. Bernard, Hooky and Terry were very, very taken with it and went out and formed a band.

PETER HOOK: Well, the funny thing was, I wasn't involved in music. I didn't know anybody that was. There were about forty, fifty people at the gig ... if that. I didn't know anybody. I didn't know anybody in the musical circle in Manchester.

JOHN BERRY: I doubt that any of the group I went with that night had aspirations to be in a band. Sure, everyone dreams of being a rock star and we were all mad about music, but I don't think they saw themselves as being in a band. They showed no musical inclination.

PETER HOOK: There was nobody that I knew there, apart from Bernard [Sumner], his wife and Terry Mason, who was a guy that I used to go to school with. I don't remember if Ian Curtis [Joy Division] was there. I can't remember if he was there or not. [Curtis missed the 4 June gig – he was to see them six weeks later on 20 July.]

TONY WILSON: So who does claim to have been there properly on that first night? Who do we know was there? Hooky and Bernard were there.

HOWARD DEVOTO: I understand some of them – because they became Joy Division eventually – were there. I mean, they weren't people I knew, so I just wouldn't know at all. I think there's a big dispute as to how many people were there that evening. I personally think there were about a hundred people.

TONY WILSON: It shows the wonderfulness of the event, the fact that the capacity is only about a hundred and fifty at the Lesser Free Trade Hall ... seven and a half thousand people claim to have been there. It's what happens at wonderful events. It's always the same. People just think they went there. I feel very privileged ... being there ... sitting there ... and gawping. Very strange.

DAWN BRADBURY: All those famous people? They weren't there. Don't be silly. It was a handful of hippies who'd gone down to see Solstice and some band from London. I don't know if Morrissey was there. That's all I'll say. Tony Wilson? I would have recognised him. He would have been the only person in the room who'd been on TV. He was on Granada News. At sixteen I would have been quite mesmerised by having a TV star in the same room. I wasn't mesmerised because I didn't see him. It was a long time ago. I wouldn't say, 'You were there and you weren't.' But it's hugely unlikely that they were.

PETER OLDHAM: I was quite impassioned about it at the time. It was pretty good. There was no stage lighting ...

the sound was pretty poor. But it was just the actual attack of the band – it had a spark to it.

TONY WILSON: As I walked out, this geezer in the black leather goes, 'What did you think of that, Mr Wilson?' I said, 'Well, Malcolm, I think ... Yeah! But the Pete Townshend stuff...' He says, 'Yeah, yeah, I know ... it's going, it's going.'

JON THE POSTMAN: My friend actually got in the lift after the gig and all the Pistols got in as well. He was very scared because, of course, he'd read the review in *NME* that at one of their London concerts there was some trouble with members of the audience, so he was a bit apprehensive ... he was also very stoned as well. But you know, they were OK.

IAIN GREY: Got home, got all my shirts out, ripped the arms off them, got rid of my flares in the bin, this was when we got back from the gig. Me and Eddie [Garrity] were like ... right, scrap all the songs, three minutes, three chords. It was just so exciting, the sheer presence of the band with Rotten. Everything I believed in about music up to that point was destroyed and rightfully so. This is the way. Sod all the Roxy Music, David Bowie: the Sex Pistols actually meant something to me, something tangible that I could do ... I could be like that, not where you've got to be in the audience. I thought, 'I can do that'. It was absolutely fantastic – a life-changing event. I was eighteen at the time.

PAUL WELSH: When we came out of the concert, I said to my girlfriend, 'I feel like I'm walking on air.' So elated. That night was the best Pistols performance I ever saw. I never got that feeling from the other punk bands I saw. After a few weeks you realised that you *had* to have been there...

PAUL MORLEY: When you came out, you knew something had happened and your body felt hot and your blood was racing and your mind was racing. But it never occurred to you that there would be any future for it. It never occurred to you that maybe every single person in that room would go on and form bands and do whatever they did. It never occurred to you because that had never happened before. It never occurred to you that anything fantastic could come from Manchester. It never occurred to you that, even though the thing we'd just seen was so fantastic, it would inspire us to do things. It was just a fantastic experience and then, much to your surprise a few days later, you found out it was going to happen again.

IAN MOSS: The only people I spoke to were on the bus going home. There were a couple of guys on the same bus who lived in Denton. I'd never seen them before. Their reaction was much the same as mine, and like many people from that time, without becoming close friends, it's something that's bonded us.

HOWARD DEVOTO: The Pistols, or John in particular, were obviously quite pleased with the reaction they got. They did their encore and he said something to the crowd like, 'Where did you all come from?' in a not unfriendly way. Malcolm said to me afterwards something like, 'Let's do it again … let's book this again.' They felt it was definitely a success. So I book the hall again – the hall were very happy to have the booking again, thirty quid. So it was duly booked for about six weeks on from then – 20 July.

MALCOLM MCLAREN: We were asked to return a second time and play with this so-called group, which I think Howard called Buzzcocks.

PAUL MORLEY: At the first show you just got the feeling that the Sex Pistols could have disappeared overnight and it would have been one of those things. But with the second show you knew that this was something titanic.

PETE SHELLEY: The whole idea was that you couldn't do such things as put on your own gigs. It was like meddling with forces beyond your control … agents and promoters knew far better. But really, it's a load of rubbish. All they do is just phone the hall, book it, get a PA in, just an afternoon's worth of phone calls and a bit of persistence and you too can be a promoter. So then the idea was to do another one.

TONY WILSON: We were dry kindling, just absolutely ready to explode into fire at that moment. Which was

Devoto's doing, to put that incendiary bomb, let alone a spark, into this community that is Manchester. It's true that people who were at the second gig claim to be at the first gig ... whatever, doesn't matter. What's important is, the Pistols happened.

HOWARD DEVOTO: Within weeks, well, certainly by the time Buzzcocks played ... I got a sticky inkling that my life had changed. I certainly know I felt a whole lot different in myself, a whole lot better in myself. Suddenly, I was engaged in something that really, really interested me.

Over the space of two hours, Solstice had ushered out the old and the Sex Pistols had ushered in the new. At the Lesser Free Trade Hall in Manchester on 4 June, the distance between the band and the audience had shrunk. The idea that being in a band was a calling that only a few wizards and technicians could aspire to had been debunked. The possibility of doing 'it' yourself – whatever that 'it' might be – was temptingly close. And it was down to the audience to make 'it' happen. Not bad for a bunch of Small Faces and Stooges cover versions. It's fortunate that the audience didn't take Rotten's advice and 'fuck off out of it', otherwise they would have missed something quite extraordinary ... and the world would be a very different place.

After the gig, *Penetration* editor Paul Welsh developed his photos. There were plenty of shots of Johnny Rotten pulling faces and Steve Jones throwing shapes. Job done. But in among the set was one photo Paul had taken from the back of the hall. It showed the Pistols in the distance; the main feature of the photo was the audience.

PAUL WELSH: When I got that photograph developed, I thought, 'Why did I take that?' You can't see the band, only the audience. If I'd had a digital camera, I would have deleted it. At the time it didn't mean anything.

'No mention of Buzzcocks at all – which was sweet of them':
A poster for the second gig, with Slaughter and the Dogs
seemingly topping the bill.   © Lesley Gilbert

CHAPTER FOUR

IT AIN'T LIKE THAT IN SHOWBIZ, IS IT?

After the Lesser Free Trade Hall gig on 4 June , the Pistols carried on with the rather haphazard live performance schedule that was becoming increasingly their norm. Off they trundled to the Black Swan in Sheffield with a debuting Clash and then to The 100 Club in London with The Damned. They planned to return to the Lesser Free Trade Hall in July. In the meantime, there was a flurry of activity in Manchester. Just as important as the first and second gigs at the Lesser Free Trade Hall in 1976 was the gap in between the two. There was organisation. There were plans. A small but noisy scattering of long-hairs at the first gig would build up to be a serious crowd for the second.

TONY WILSON: Maybe it's only in a small city that you have that kind of communication that can take you from thirty five people on 4 June to several hundred on 20 July. The word goes out, the word spreads.

PETER HOOK: I think the people that saw the first Sex Pistols' gig – in the same way that we did – walked out of it, did something and then went and told whoever they knew about it and it just came on from there. So by the time you got to the second one there were more bands than Soft Mick. There were literally forty, sixty, eighty, a hundred bands. Everybody was forming a band. For me, it changed. Literally, the next day. It was overnight and I went round telling everybody I knew about the Sex Pistols.

For the uninitiated, 'Soft Mick' is a Mancunian/Lancastrian expression that acts as an 'intensifier'. As in: 'She has more fur coats than Soft Mick.' So, Soft Mick is used as the benchmark for someone who has a lot of something. Don't say you haven't learned something...

STEVE DIGGLE: The day after the Pistols' gig we had a rehearsal at Howard's. All plugged into one amp – bass, guitar, vocals – all screaming out. Like Yeats said, it had 'a terrible beauty'. From the first rehearsal we had a chemistry. We didn't have to rehearse like other groups.

IAN MOSS: I was evangelical about it, honestly. I told everybody about that band – everybody I encountered – about the Sex Pistols.

PAUL MORLEY: I've no idea of the time difference between the first and the second show, but I just get the feeling that we'd all run around and said, 'You've got to come, you've got to come, this is amazing, they're actually playing.' And by then, the myth of the Sex Pistols had got bigger and it was clearly a more obviously dramatic thing that was happening. Whereas I got the feeling the first thing was almost on the quiet ... there was almost like a rumour of a rumour when they came that first time. They were clearly very obscure, although the *NME* was writing about them. The whole power of the Pistols' myth was beginning to happen and the Pistols themselves already looked like something had happened to them. You got the feeling that the second time they were beginning to change physically and mentally and they knew they were part of something and that energy was transmitted a lot more the second time than the first time.

PETE SHELLEY: I suppose it ended up being a different kind of following. People, instead of just being passive observers of the culture, became active participants and started forming their own bands. Just doing basically what they were doing anyway ... but accelerated. I think it was the fact that nobody was stopping them doing it.

PETER HOOK: It was that immediate; it was like somebody opening a door in a darkened room.

TONY WILSON: I was a big Van Morrison fan, but afterwards I'd gone to visit an old girlfriend in London. She said, 'What do you think of the new Van Morrison album?' and I'd go, 'Pardon? Who cares, the world has turned, it's all moved on.' The most wonderful moments grow from that single spark.

IAIN GREY: Going to see the Pistols, that was the catalyst. Suddenly, overnight, we thought, 'Right, tear the sleeves off our shirts, get your hair cut, this is it!'

PETER HOOK: Literally the next day, I went to Mazel's in Manchester and bought a bass guitar for thirty five quid. [Mazel Radio was a music and electrical second-hand shop near Manchester's Piccadilly train station]. I went in and said, 'Can I have a bass guitar?' and he went, 'Well, here's one. Thirty five quid.' Give him thirty five quid and walked out with the guitar and thought, 'What the bloody hell am I going to do with this?' So I went to a music shop on Deansgate and bought a book on how to play rock 'n' roll bass guitar: *Play In A Day*.

JOHN BERRY: He may well have done. He's rewritten his history a little bit. I'm sure it happened *fairly* soon after that. It certainly lit the blue touchpaper.

Peter Hook set about the business of 'rehearsing' with his friend – and later band mate in Joy Division and New Order – Bernard Sumner, who'd also been to the Pistols' gig. Sumner already had a guitar and an amp but, so far, hadn't managed to do a great deal with it. After the Pistols' gig, that quickly changed.

TERRY MASON: I wasn't quick enough. I should have got the bass. I got a guitar and an amp from the '£10 and under section' of the *Manchester Evening News*. Hofner Strat copy, strings caked in rust. Barney [Bernard] used to get pissed off that I couldn't play the chords that he could.

PETER HOOK: We didn't have an amp. Bernard wired up his gran's gramophone with four wires connecting my bass guitar and his guitar to her gramophone ... and we played through that. She went mad when she came home ... we'd ruined her gramophone.

TERRY MASON: Not quite. They were using Barney's amp with both guitars in. Bernard was sufficiently wise to know that, if you put bass frequencies through it, it wouldn't last long. Bernard read up somewhere about valve radios and found one at his gran's. He made Hooky use that.

JOHN BERRY: People in my peer group didn't aspire to be in bands. In our group we wanted to see people who we *couldn't* be. That's why we loved Bowie and Roxy and Lou Reed, because they were from another planet and they were beautiful and we weren't beautiful. We were fucking skint and we had bad clothes. And bad teeth. Mind you, having bad teeth never stopped Bowie.

Elsewhere, another enticing possibility was slowly gathering momentum: that of putting the Pistols on television. A few hundred yards away from the Lesser Free Trade Hall was Granada Television and that's where the plot was being hatched. Tony Wilson – regardless of whether he really was at the first gig – was desperate to get the Pistols onto his new show. Wilson actually wanted his own politics show but he was seen as being unreliable and lacking in research capabilities. The fact that he carried a pouch full of marijuana with him at all times didn't help bolster his political credibility. The politics job was given to Wilson's colleague Gordon Burns – as a result Tony wouldn't speak to Burns for the best part of a year. As compensation, Wilson was given the task of expanding the ten-minute music-and-arts slot he already had into a fully-fledged programme. It was to be called *So It Goes*. Acts like Tom Waits and The Chieftains had already been booked and Wilson had filmed an item with KISS backstage at the Free Trade Hall. Wilson sensed that punk was about to make the show look like yesterday's news, so he took action.

TONY WILSON: The night after I saw the Pistols, I went running to my boss and said, 'Chris, Chris, saw this band last night, got to have them on, fantastic, fantastic,' screaming, shouting ... 'Doesn't matter that they're not signed, they're fantastic,' blah, blah, blah.

CHRIS PYE (Producer – *So It Goes*): Tony came through the door and said, 'Hey man! I saw this great gig...' Tony didn't describe things in detail most of the time. Tony just came in with a kind of wave of enthusiasm. It's the enthusiasm that drove us really.

TONY WILSON: Chris Pye wasn't having any of this, so he said, 'Right, well, you've got to take Malcolm Clarke, your researcher, who is a responsible human being – not like you – take him to see the band and we'll see what he thinks.'

PETER WALKER (Director – *So It Goes*): I can remember from the very early stage in the series, perhaps episode one of the whole series, Tony Wilson decided that he wanted to try and get a group like the Sex Pistols on the show ... because that was more of what he saw the future of music was going to be. The stuff we were getting was very fringy, obviously because there were other programmes that did the mainstream music and we always tried to make sure that it was always good music.

TONY WILSON: All that summer, it was the last great heat wave. It's really weird to think that punk, with its boredom and industrial mentality, came in that fantastic summer. So, on a fantastically hot, wonderful sunny afternoon, we drove to Walthamstow [in London] and parked outside the gig about eight o'clock, a bright wonderful blue sky. We walked into this massive civic hall that was completely dark and kind of quite cool. At the far end, this racket was coming off the stage and you could see about twenty people, who were all in like a semi-circle. As we got nearer, the reason it was a semi-circle was because that was the gobbing distance. John [Johnny Rotten] was gobbing as hard as he could, so that's why this little audience of about twenty five people were just out of gobbing range. And they were stunning.

JORDAN: It's very difficult to say exactly why the Pistols were so strong. The only thing I can think is that very rarely you get a bunch of people that come together that just make a unit and all have the same attitude. Quite often, things are very preconceived, especially these days, they're very much a product of producers and managers.

GLEN MATLOCK: We went everywhere just to get some gigs, just to get a bit of stagecraft together. We played this Conservative club once, and we're hammering away and a guy kept coming in to tell us to turn down a little bit. And a little bit more. And in the end he said, 'No good lads, we'll pay you, but you'll just have to stop because they can't hear the bingo in the next room.'

JORDAN: One of my funniest occasions was when the Pistols were playing the Pier at Hastings, which is right on the south coast of England. There's a little sort of domed area at the back, which usually some organist would be playing in the summer season. Malcolm had got them booked in there and Sid [Vicious – not then in the band] and I went down by train to see the Pistols on this pier. Nearly the whole audience were German, Italian and Swedish tourists all down there for their summer hols. It was absolutely bizarre.

Meanwhile, Paul Welsh got his photos and review of the first Pistols gig into issue eight of *Penetration* magazine. With American rockers KISS on the cover, the issue – costing 12p – also featured Hawkwind, *The Rocky Horror Picture Show*, as well as his piece on the Pistols. Under the headline ROTTEN VOCALIST OF THE YEAR NO. 1, Welsh submitted his on-the-spot report: 'They blitzed the audience with power chords and vocals set in a different key to the music,' he wrote. 'When I saw them they whipped the audience to a frenzy with ease and, when responded to, Johnny Rotten actually smiled! Sex Pistols are, at the moment, unique and they're amazing live, but I'll leave you to form your own opinions, see them soon.'

PAUL WELSH: I wanted to start integrating punk bands into the magazine. A lot of people who read it didn't like the punk element. I could see a connection between rock, heavy metal and punk. Back then, people couldn't see it. The magazine came out in between the two concerts. It wasn't a very professional review. I did my best to try to give people an idea of what the gig was like.

PAUL MORLEY: I was doing a fanzine at that time. I'd started to put it together before I'd seen the Pistols or the Ramones or Patti Smith. So it'd had Dylan in it, and it had T. Rex in it and it had Ted Nugent. I had to change very quickly in mid-flow. It still had Bob Dylan on the cover, because I'd printed a lot of them and I'd paid for it, so I couldn't afford to redo it, but very quickly I rammed in a little bit about the Pistols and a bit about The Stranglers. Now I don't know which one I reviewed, I get a feeling I reviewed the first one but I don't know unfortunately. I was young. I didn't put much detail into the review, which I wish I had done now.

Elsewhere, punk was taking hold in Manchester – you were either for it or against it. With no access to King's Road clobber, the Mancunian candidates had to make do with what they had.

PETER HOOK: I was wearing a dog collar and having my hair spiked up and wearing army boots. People literally would stop in the street and trip over. You'd be putting soap in your hair to make it stick up. Me and Bernard [Sumner] used to go to buy Scout shirts and paint swastikas on them and put SS badges on and all that crap. God, you wouldn't be allowed anywhere near it now! It was funny.

DAWN BRADBURY: It was like a musical version of *Lord of the Flies* – punks in Manchester were a group. The core group of punks in Manchester was probably about thirty people ... with three thousand on the periphery.

STEVE DIGGLE: We must have been the first punks on the block. Howard looked weird. Pete looked weird. I remember standing at the bus stop in a black coat and black cord trousers – which, incidentally, were flares which were sewn in because you couldn't buy them – and people were like, 'Look at him with straight legs on.' During that interim period between the two gigs, people didn't know what punk was. The only reason we knew was because of the Sex Pistols and because the Ramones' album had come out. We were waiting for this next gig to happen in a few weeks, building up to it, wondering what was going to happen as a result.

As the 20 July gig approached, another band was added to the bill, above Buzzcocks: Slaughter And The Dogs. Wayne Barrett, Mike (Mick) Rossi, Howard 'Zip' Bates, Mike 'Spider' Day and Brian 'Mad Muffet' Grantham were a bunch of glam-rock toughs from Wythenshawe, one of Europe's biggest housing estates and certainly the noisiest, with its proximity to Manchester Airport. They were local heroes on their estate but, by getting a slot at the Lesser Free Trade Hall, Slaughter had broken out of south Manchester and bagged themselves a gig in the city centre – a big deal at the time.

HOWARD 'ZIP' BATES (bass player – Slaughter And The Dogs): We all came from the council estate of Wythenshawe. People say it was rough. You only know what you know – it was certainly deprived. There wasn't a lot of money around. I remember seeing my first electric guitar in Woolworths. It was like something from another planet. It cost about twenty four quid and you'd look at it and go ... wow! I joined the band through Slaughter guitarist Mike Day. He said, 'I'm in a band and they're looking for a bass player, do you play?' I said no, never played in my life. I played brass not bass. He said, 'Do you fancy it?' and I said ... 'Why not?' So I went down to A1 [music shop] in Manchester, picked up a £20 Jazz bass copy – that's the one I used at the Pistols' gig. I spent a month going to Spider's house learning how to play then my first gig I did was at a pub in Manchester called the Mountain Ash in 1975. I was fifteen.

WAYNE BARRETT (lead singer – Slaughter And The Dogs): All there was to do in Wythenshawe was hang around the chippy, go round on your pushbike, a lot of people robbing, silly things like that. Nothing. Mike [Rossi] and myself, we'd go down to the press factory when they distributed all the newspapers, like four, five in the morning, to pick up the *New Musical Express*, *Sounds* and everything. That filled us in with the Pistols' information and things like that.

Slaughter And The Dogs and Buzzcocks were chalk and cheese – and they grated against each other immediately. The first thing the Bolton Institute Bohemians did when they found out Slaughter had been added to the bill was check out the competition from the council-estate kids.

HOWARD DEVOTO: I tended to be the one on the blower, but Pete was helping out all along ... getting the group together, organising the gig, going along to check out Slaughter And The Dogs. We did travel out to Wythenshawe and saw them play. Slaughter And The Dogs turned out to be kind of Bowie and Roxy kids. We thought, 'Oh, we hadn't quite realised you were like this.'

WAYNE BARRETT: They came to my mum's place ... I always remember my mum was scared to death when she saw Pete Shelley all dressed up and everything.

PETE SHELLEY: They [Slaughter And The Dogs] always used to think they were the best. We knew that *thinking* that you're the best doesn't necessarily mean you *are* the best. So we were more philosophical about the dispute. As a result they saw us as being rivals and as a result lost the plot completely.

WAYNE BARRETT: Everybody we met, they said, 'Where are you playing next?' We just said, 'We're playing in the Lesser Free Trade Hall.' So they said, 'When?' And we gave them the information.

Slaughter had already been making noises south of the city and they went about the business of getting themselves noticed further afield. Something which they proved to be remarkably adept at.

TONY WILSON: Martin Hannett, the young Manchester nascent genius producer who I'd begun to know, insisted that I go to a gig in 'The Shed' I think it was called, in Portwood in Stockport on 15 May 1976 – this is two and a half weeks before the Pistols – to see Slaughter And The Dogs. It was weird, a bit Bowie-esque ... wearing dresses and playing vacuum cleaners. It was weird and it was different and it wasn't like any of that crap that we were putting out.

EDDIE GARRITY: I went to school with Mike Rossi and then he got expelled. He went to another school and met Wayne Barrett. So we were going to start a band before he formed Slaughter And The Dogs. Then later I joined them anyway. We were in a band called Wild Ram then. I think it was more the fans of each band who were more rivals. Before we went on stage the leads would be cut and things like that. We'd each go to each other's gigs to see what the other one was up to and then, if there was anything good, we'd copy it. They were like our rival band in Wythenshawe. We got together to do a gig at The Forum and Tony Wilson off the telly came along to that one, to do the introductions. He mentioned that we were both part of this new punk movement for some reason. So obviously that's why we went to the second gig 'cause we'd already been pulled into it.

PETE SHELLEY: Me and Howard were grammar-school boys, so it wasn't really the sound of the terraces. I mean, me and Howard read books and things like that.

MICK ROSSI (guitarist – Slaughter And The Dogs): We went to Sharston High School...

I interviewed Mick Rossi and Wayne Barrett together. They are a double act. Rossi is small in stature and as rake thin as he was forty years ago. You have to call him Mick – only Barrett gets to call him Mike. Barrett is beefy, his leather strides straining to contain his hefty frame. When reading this, be aware that Rossi now speaks with a strong American accent. When I asked him to identify himself for the tape, he replied, 'Mick Rossi – guitar player and full-time dreamer.' Wayne Barrett, his 'other half', has retained his Mancunian twang, despite living in France for many years. Their act is even funnier if you read it in your head with those accents in mind.

WAYNE BARRETT: I was in music school doing music lessons. I was playing bass at that time. I met up with Mike [Mick Rossi] in the schoolyard. After that we started hanging out together and then we decided to start a band off ... dreams of Bowie, Roxy Music, Alice Cooper, Slade ... all the 1970s glam stuff. We were told at school by our headmaster, Mr Muscott, 'If you're still alive and still kicking...

MICK ROSSI: Jesus, a blast from the past...

WAYNE BARRETT: ...he got us into his room once and he said to us that we'd all end up on the dole. Or in prison. And we wouldn't ever work...

MICK ROSSI: That's encouragement for ya, right?

WAYNE BARRETT: If you're in school and somebody says that to you, what do you want us to do – kill ourselves? We just said, 'We're going make something out of ourselves,' and that pushed us on.

MICK ROSSI: We used to rehearse in his [Barrett's] mum's front room. We'd take the budgie cage off and then the stand became the mic stand. I had a shitty little guitar, so we kind of bummed around doing that for a little bit.

WAYNE BARRETT: The first band was called Wayne Barrett And The Mime Troop.

MICK ROSSI: There was nothing – literally *nothing* – in Wythenshawe; just Labour clubs and people singing Tom Jones impersonations. And bingo. That's how we started off; we started doing the Labour clubs as

Slaughter And The Dogs and doing a whole bunch of covers. We started writing, basically right away, but that was eye opening, doing the Labour clubs. We used to do two sets and I think we got paid fifteen quid. Which was a lot of money then. We'd all pile into the back of a van, it would be our set – and then it would be the bingo, which was the highlight of the evening – and then our second set.

WAYNE BARRETT: One night at a Conservative club, there was this big fat lad who introduced us: 'The Slaughtered Dog, playing here tonight.' So we went on stage to round about forty people whose average age was eighty five. We did the four songs and...

MICK ROSSI: Came off...

WAYNE BARRETT: 'Look, I'll pay you...'

MICK ROSSI: 'Go home ... sod off.'

WAYNE BARRETT: You've got to imagine the Wythenshawe situation. At that time it was like ... it was *hell*. Everything was unemployment, unemployment, unemployment. There was robbing all over the place. When you write a song in that kind of environment, you can't say, 'I love you, I love you, I love you.' It's got to be a little bit angry. We didn't set out to be punks.

MICK ROSSI: Before we started doing covers, we actually wrote a song called 'Love, Speed And Beer'. That was the first song we ever wrote.

WAYNE BARRETT: The punk thing – we didn't really know what the punk thing meant. We were just banging on the guitar and yelling our heads off, basically saying, 'Listen to us.' But we were wary about what was happening in London.

MICK ROSSI: There was such a lack of activity in Manchester at the time – in terms of new bands and new blood – so anything that was coming in was great.

IAIN GREY: I used to go to school with Mick Rossi. There was one time going to a music store in Manchester. He hadn't warned me, but he had a guitar case with him – which I thought had a guitar in. So in we go, he picks up this Fender Stratocaster, puts it in the case and walks out. The woman had seen what he done and he just said to me, 'Run!' I get home, the police are at my house. Mick's buried it in his garden. He left it there for six or seven months till he thought it was safe to dig up. That's the way they were. Wythenshawe scallies.

WAYNE BARRETT: We'd go into Mike's [Rossi's] bedroom or into mine. You'd get the guitar, bash a few chords out and then get paper and a pen ... and see what happens.

Opinion on Slaughter And The Dogs has always been divided. They were either the authentic howl of council-estate teen anger or a bunch of glam-rock chancers out to jump on the bandwagon. But didn't *everyone* jump on the punk bandwagon? Joe Strummer left pub rockers The 101ers after seeing the Pistols – without that bit of bandwagon-jumping there'd be no Clash.

TONY WILSON: To be honest, if I have to stand here and say, 'Would you rather have Slaughter And The Dogs or The Damned as the build-up to this cultural revolution?' I'd rather have Slaughter And The Dogs. I'd rather have Wythenshawe.

MICK ROSSI: We did a show at The Forum [a civic venue in Wythenshawe's main precinct] and Wayne's look then ... he came on with patent decorating pants, a pair of sneakers, an old jacket with the *Guardian* in his pocket, a waistcoat, a watch and a ratty old shirt. That would be classed as punk I guess, in today's terms, but it was just sort of something that happened. We did the Wythenshawe Forum, which is a real big place. It was unheard of and it was promoted by our manager, so it was off our own back that we did that.

WAYNE BARRETT: If there's a fifth member of the group, it's got to be Ray [Rossi, manager] because he was the real backbone of the band. He kept us together for ages because we'd be in the rehearsal room and, after the third song, we'd be beating the shit out of each other basically. Because we were kids. He gave us a lot of guidance; he always had good vision. Ray did a lot, our manager.

MICK ROSSI: My brother at the time.

WAYNE BARRETT: He still is your brother...

MICK ROSSI: Hey, Ray, how you doin'?

So the stage was set for the next visit by the Pistols to the Lesser Free Trade Hall. Buzzcocks, for their first real gig, were bottom of the bill, with Slaughter And The Dogs on next. Buzzcocks had made some hand-stencilled posters of their own flagging up all three bands. Slaughter And The Dogs went to the trouble of producing some highly professional-looking, but somewhat misleading, posters. Their version has the Sex Pistols underneath Slaughter And The Dogs.

HOWARD BATES: It was the biggest thing we'd ever done. We'd just been doing our little local circuit. Then the other guys got hold of McLaren to organise the gig. They came back one day and said, We're going to do a gig at the Lesser Free Trade Hall with this new band ... they only had twenty or thirty people the last time they played, so if we can get on the bill we can pack it out for you, because we had a local following in

Wythenshawe, even though we were a covers band with a few originals thrown in. We organised the tickets and posters, hence on some of the posters we're above the Pistols. That's just Wythenshawe cheek innit? Having balls.

HOWARD DEVOTO: I remember a great deal of confidence on the part of Slaughter. A lot of front and sort of ... rubbish, really. They produced these posters with Slaughter And The Dogs up here [top of the poster] and Sex Pistols down there, no mention of Buzzcocks at all. Which was sweet of them.

HOWARD BATES: We did mention them. It says 'plus support'...

HOWARD DEVOTO: Punk was never a loving world, with everybody blissed-out together and being jolly supportive. It ain't like that in showbiz, is it?

EDDIE GARRITY: We were desperate to get on to that bill because the publicity was building for it and there was a lot of media interest. There was talk about getting Buzzcocks out of the way, trying to find their address to go down and beat them up so they couldn't play. We were even going to wait outside on the night and do it, you know but we got talked out of it [laughing]. Then they said we could roadie instead so we settled for that. Ray [Rossi] was organising it so there was no point in trying to get them off the bill. Ray was pretty heavy anyway, so we left them alone.

PETE SHELLEY: Mick Rossi thought that Slaughter And The Dogs were the best band in all the world and they could get in twenty million people and sell all these tickets. They blagged Malcolm into doing the show with them as the second band.

HOWARD BATES: There was a lot of bullshitting going on – we were all into football and, if we were talking to a red [Manchester United fan], we'd say that United goalkeeper Alex Stepney is going to introduce us. If they were a blue, we said some City player was going to do it. We shifted a lot of tickets! That's why it was packed out.

STEVE DIGGLE: I don't know how they got on the bill. I think it was something to do with Howard. If it was left to me I'd have fucking kicked their arses. They were seventeen – we were twenty.

So with cheeky posters all made up and Buzzcocks thankfully left unmolested, the stage was set for the Pistols' return. The event was booked into the diary for the Lesser Free Trade Hall as 'Sex Pistols etc, 6–10.30'. A £26 deposit had been paid and Mr McLaren and Howard Trafford were listed as the contacts. There was a genuine sense of excitement across the city about the second gig – something was stirring; something was happening. What's more, the price of entry to the Lesser Free Trade Hall to see the Sex Pistols had doubled in the space of six weeks.

To £1.

LESSER FREE TRADE HALL
FREE TRADE HALL-PETER ST MANCHESTER
£1·00 TUESDAY 20th JULY 7·30pm £1·00
SEX PISTOLS
WITH SLAUGHTER
AND THE DOGS
BUT BUZZCOCKS
TICKETS AT FREE TRADE HALL £1·00 BOOKING OFFICE

Hand-stencilled flyer made by the rather frustrated Buzzcocks,
this time listing the full line-up.   © *Howard Devoto*

LESSER FREE TRADE HALL
MANCHESTER

SLAUGHTER & THE DOGS
★
THE SEX PISTOLS
★
plus support
TUESDAY, 20th JULY, 1976
at 7.30 p.m.

Ticket £1   Admits one

'With the second show, you knew that this was something
titanic': A ticket for the second gig (with no mention, once
again, of Buzzcocks…). Note the doubling in price.

© *Paul Burgess Archive*

CHAPTER FIVE

SEX PISTOLS, ETC.

The second Sex Pistols gig at the Lesser Free Trade Hall, on 20 July 1976, was the logical culmination of the activity sparked by the first show. In the space of just six weeks, the lads who took the money on the door, printed the tickets and played records during the interval had worked themselves into a band ... Buzzcocks. No 'The' ... just *Buzzcocks*. To this day, Shelley can still take sizeable exception if you wrongly refer to his band as 'The' Buzzcocks. The band's line-up: Howard Devoto on vocals, Pete Shelley on guitar, Steve Diggle on bass and sixteen-year-old John Maher on drums.

JOHN MAHER (drummer – Buzzcocks): I remember Howard coming 'round to my house. I'd just come back from school having done an O Level in the morning and

I was due to go back to do another one in the afternoon. He'd turned up in my lunch hour. He wanted to know if I was interested in coming along and doing a rehearsal with his band. That must have happened just after that first Free Trade Hall gig. I wasn't aware of the Pistols at this point. The whole point was to get a band ready in time to play on 20 July. I joined Buzzcocks about four weeks before the second Pistols gig.

HOWARD DEVOTO: If the gig in June had been the detonation, that second gig was the cloud and noise where everybody knew something was going off. It was sold out. As far as I remember, it was packed. There was a Slaughter And The Dogs contingent. We didn't have a contingent, apart from a few mates turning up.

TONY WILSON: The twentieth of July, I was away. I took a week's holiday in France, my first holiday for about a year. So I didn't go to the second gig. I got back and they said it was fantastic and Buzzcocks played and there were thousands of people ... whatever.

DICK WITTS (musician – Granada TV presenter): I went with Tony to see the Sex Pistols – the second one in July. He went with me and my girlfriend.

PAUL WELSH: I saw Tony Wilson there. I was walking across the back of the hall and Wilson was coming in the opposite direction. He had pink sunglasses on and a chiffon scarf. He said, 'Have you seen Malcolm, man?' I knew Tony Wilson used to read my magazine, *Penetration*. He never bought it, he just used to go into Virgin Records and read it.

PETE SHELLEY: For the second gig we actually made posters. We had posters made and went around and stuck them up ourselves in the middle of the night. It actually brought enough people together that they could look around and recognise each other [from the first gig] so, the next time they met, they had that thing in common.

MARK E. SMITH: We met up in a pub round the corner: Cox's Bar. We were all going, 'Shall we go, shan't we go? Sounds a bit naff to me, it's from London.' It had to be American for us. Malcolm McLaren walked into the pub – into the vault – and he had this leather suit on ... big ginger hair ... winkle pickers. Pretty unusual in those days. He came over to us and said, 'Are you coming over to see the band?' It really impressed me – a good management style that. Impressive. So we decided to go. And it was good.

PETER OLDHAM: There were all these A&R men dressed in jeans and carrying attaché cases, all queuing to sign the Pistols up. I think I remember seeing Tony Wilson there then. It was more of an event, there was a bit more of a buzz about it. It was gathering momentum.

GARY AINSLEY (audience member): I'd sort of been into Northern Soul because I came from Oldham. There was this great idea that in the Northern Soul venues you changed into your posing gear, came out of the toilets, got onto the dance floor and performed.

LORRAINE JOYCE (audience member): We used to wear things like pencil skirts, stilettos. We used to wear straight-legged jeans, which I know now sounds absolutely nothing, but everybody was in big flares and kipper ties.

GARY AINSLEY: A friend of mine rang me up. He said, 'Do you fancy seeing this punk band?' I said, 'What's punk?' Nobody had heard of punk. He said, 'They wear ripped T-shirts' ... and as soon as he said 'ripped T-shirts' I thought, 'Right, I'm going'. After the concert I just came out and you just knew it was just going to be so huge. It was so different to anything.

STEVE 'SHY' BURKE (audience member – fanzine writer): I was a bit of football hooligan, following United all over the place. I suppose I was what you'd call a soul boy. I was into heavy funk like Rufus, Brass Construction and The Fatback Band. I wasn't into Bowie or Roxy like everyone else, but I did like Mott The Hoople, Alex Harvey ... my mind was open. I used to work at a building firm – I was a glazier. Sometimes they'd send an apprentice painter and decorator with me, who happened to be Wayne Barrett. He said, 'I'm in a band and I've got a gig coming up. He kept mithering [bothering] me to buy a ticket. I bought one just to shut him up. I'd never heard of the Sex Pistols. I'd never bought the *NME*. But we went. And my life changed.

WAYNE BARRETT: The gig, as it went for us, was just like doing a Labour club basically, except it was a little bit bigger and we were playing at the back of the Free Trade Hall, where we saw the big bands like Bowie ... Mick Ronson.

MICK ROSSI: My hero, Mick Ronson ... [Slaughter And The Dogs took part of their name from *Slaughter On 10th Avenue*, Ronson's 1974 debut solo album. The rest of it comes from David Bowie's *Diamond Dogs* from the same year.]

WAYNE BARRETT: We loved following Ronno [Mick Ronson]. The punk movement – with the Pistols – we'd read about it.

MICK ROSSI: We were aware of it.

For those who like to argue about what punk rock is really all about – the Situationists vs the Boot Boys, if you will – witness the bubbling feud between Howard and Pete's Bohemian Buzzcocks and the low-rent Slaughter And The Dogs. The whole debate encapsulated by an enmity between two bands that is as strong today as it was in 1976.

PETE SHELLEY: They didn't sell all the tickets that they said they would. They just blagged themselves on to the bill – but we bided our time.

MICK ROSSI: We had the majority of the crowd there, 'cause the first time the Pistols played there, there was like thirty or so. Second time, it was packed. We had a little mob that used to follow us around – they were great.

JON THE POSTMAN: Oh, they brought roughly ten or fifteen people with them, because there were all these wimpy young sort of girls and blokes waving flags about as if it was a Bay City Rollers gig, which me and my friends found totally horrendous and disgusting. We hated them ever since.

WAYNE BARRETT: I knew, let's say 80 per cent of the people that were there, because there were a lot of people from Wythenshawe.

VANESSA CORLEY (audience member): We lived in Wythenshawe. They played at The Forum at Wythenshawe. To then go to play at the Lesser Free Trade Hall, this was quite a big step up from the little local haunt. So that was why we went to see them.

PAUL WELSH: We hated Slaughter And The Dogs. There used to be a kids' programme on at the time with a band called Flintlock. They reminded me of them. They didn't seem like a punk band.

LORRAINE JOYCE: A friend asked me to go because Slaughter And The Dogs were doing it. I'd never heard of punk, nobody knew what punk was. But it wasn't for me. I mean, I actually don't like punk rock. I loved the gay clubs. I loved the music in the gay clubs.

IAIN GREY: Slaughter And The Dogs brought along a load of David Bowie/Roxy Music fans. So there were these punks and these Bowie/Roxy fans and there was this big fight. They were like a cabaret version of punk, Slaughter And The Dogs. They weren't credible, they were like an embarrassment. Because we hadn't got anywhere with our band [Wild Ram with Eddie Garrity] and they were the first ones to kind of make it from Wythenshawe. So we were quite jealous.

JON THE POSTMAN: Oh, we thought they were awful, we thought they were sort of a tenth-rate glam-rock band … it was horrendous and not interesting at all.

STEVE SHY: Slaughter And The Dogs … they were just a little rock band trying to make it. People say they jumped on the bandwagon. *Everybody* jumped on the bandwagon. Pete and Howard hadn't done anything before they saw the Pistols. I'm never going to call [have a go at] Slaughter And The Dogs for that.

EDDIE GARRITY: There was no image in the audience at the second gig. But by then, nobody knew what punk was, so there was a mixture of hippies, just normally dressed people, you know and there'd be a few weird looking people, so it was right across the board. Because I'd been going to gigs around then and they'd all be dressed in your Slade gear or whatever, the Bowie kids and the Roxy kids, this was just totally, totally new, you know – a bit of everything really.

WAYNE BARRETT: There was a message. The only message that we had at that time was getting the kids off the streets and having a good time. Watching a local band, basically, rather than going stealing cars.

MICK ROSSI: We got a little bit of press, which filtered back to London. We were really popular at the time in Wythenshawe and Manchester and our popularity was growing.

JOHN MAHER: There seemed to be a bit of antagonism coming from Slaughter And The Dogs, a bit of an attitude from their camp. They did the thing with printing posters for the gig but they left our name off. I got the impression they thought they should be top of the bill. A bit of typical bullshit, musician ego going on. It was my first gig – I hadn't experienced that before. There was certainly no sense of camaraderie between Slaughter And The Dogs and ourselves.

TONY WILSON: The reason why Slaughter And The Dogs did not seem to be the punk thing was the glam element. They probably had a little bit too much Bowie and a little too much Mick Ronson, but nevertheless, they were good. Let's get back to music and tribute the late genius Mr Hannett [Martin Hannett, producer of Slaughter And The Dogs' first single, 'Cranked Up Really High', who also produced Buzzcocks, Magazine, U2 and Joy Division – he died in 1991)]. 'Cranked Up Really High' is one of the great punk records, it really is. When you get Jesus, you get quite a few John the Baptists; not the real thing, but leading to the real thing. Let's put them down as one of the John the Baptists.

IAN MOSS: Slaughter And The Dogs were a cabaret band, basically. They were kind of the back end of glam rock. They wanted to be rock stars.

MICK ROSSI: Manchester at the time, it was still the big bands that seemed to be so unreachable. It was so far away they were like living [on] Mars. Seeing the Sex Pistols sound check had a profound effect on me. We'd done our sound check and it was great, we were all happy. And then the Pistols had their sound check and Steve Jones sorted the chords of 'Anarchy' ... [singing] DA-DA DEH DEH DA-DA DEH DEH...

I thought, 'That sounds fucking good'. John [Rotten] had a cold at the time and he got the lyrics out of his pocket on a horrible, dirty old snotty bit of paper.

GLEN MATLOCK: I liked Slaughter And The Dogs. I thought they were a fun kind of band. I didn't really consider them to be a punk band, although they got involved in that 'cause that was what was going on at the time. I became quite friendly with Rossi over the years. I found that he was really coming more from like the Spiders From Mars thing. Mick Ronson took him under his wing and he was heavily influenced by that period of the Bowie thing. Which was a cool place to come from, but everything became punk. Sometimes you have to jump on the coach, wherever it's going. Whether it's going to where you want to go or not.

PETER HOOK: They were too cocky for me, Slaughter And The Dogs. I didn't like them. They were too arrogant; they were like these little wide boys. We used to share a practice place and Slaughter And The Dogs used to wait for all the bands to go home and they used to go and steal your gear. You'd come in and ... bleedin' 'ell, Slaughter And The Dogs have done it again!

IAIN GREY: Oh God, they were right tealeaves. They were from Wythenshawe.

So, opinion on Slaughter And The Dogs still tends to divide people. But one thing was certain: on the run-up to the 20 July gig, the band were planning to give the show everything they'd got.

MICK ROSSI: We were thrilled. This is where Bowie played. This is where Lou Reed did 'White Heat'. This is where Ronson did *Slaughter On 10th Avenue*. Just to be under the same roof as that...

WAYNE BARRETT: All the good – all the *great* artists from the 1970s ... So we were doing our mini-concert of what they were doing basically. That's how I saw the gig.

Some of the people who attended the first Pistols' performance decided to come back for more. As well as the 100-per cent increase in the ticket price, they found a somewhat fuller Lesser Free Trade Hall than they'd witnessed six weeks earlier. This time around, 121 tickets were sold. One other thing had changed too – the peace-and-love vibe created by Geoff and the Solstice boys would prove to be sorely missing. Gig number two was shaping up to be an altogether more aggressive affair.

PAUL MORLEY: I remember the first one being a sparse audience of people, very still and quite sober. I remember the second one having much more of a charge in the atmosphere, a much more exciting place to be. You got the sense that people like me that had gone on their own the first time definitely brought people back and said, 'You have got to see this, you will not believe this.'

JOHN MAHER: I remember when the Pistols turned up in afternoon – they all appeared at the back of the hall.

That was quite an eye-opener for me. The way they were dressed. The swagger that they had. It certainly made me sit up and take notice.

PETER OLDHAM: Of course, the great Malcolm McLaren was there as well. He took the money on the door.

PETE SHELLEY: McLaren brought up a bus-load of journalists to witness what was happening.

HOWARD DEVOTO: Certainly the Pistols bandwagon was going by the time of the second gig: Malcolm had the clout. People were latching on to how hip it all was and he was able to get some of the music journalists who were latching on to it: Caroline Coon [*Melody Maker*], Jonh Ingham [*Sounds*], certainly I remember them being there that night.

WAYNE BARRETT: Malcolm was walking around with black leathers on and red slippers. It was like a Quentin Crisp kind of thing.

PETER HOOK: It was the second one that actually started the scene in Manchester, where everybody started getting involved with each other. The Drones and The Fall and everybody started mixing after the second one. The audience reaction at the first concert was quite quiet, they weren't going mad. By the time they got to the second one, that was when all the fighting started.

MARK E. SMITH: There was a big split in the audience, that second time, between the punks – before it was punk, that is – and the glam-rock lot. We were very anti-glam rock. To us it was sort of 'regular' ... Bowie covers ... just crap. You think these things are serious when you're a teenager, don't you?

HOWARD DEVOTO: At that second gig, people were either getting what the Sex Pistols and ourselves were trying to achieve, or were prepared to give it a damn good go. There was the vibe that there was something seriously happening now. Six weeks between the gigs and the bandwagon had rolled on for them quite a lot, so it was feeling like a bigger event all round.

PAUL MORLEY: There were like midgets dressed in bondage gear, which is the most *avant garde* thing you can ever imagine because forty years later that would still kind of scare you. This was very strange, like out of some weird kind of science-fiction film. The Sex Pistols' entourage gathered at the front, kind of snooty about the strange Manchester people, because, in a sense, compared to what the Sex Pistols and their entourage looked like, we did have cloth caps and clogs on.

GARY AINSLEY: Well, as far as I can remember, it sort of broke out in serious violence and there was a lot of chair-smashing. I think the Sex Pistols had brought some groupies with them that weren't from Manchester.

JOHN MAHER: I fully expected myself to be nervous. The only thing I could compare it to is when I'd done a school concert – I'd persuaded the school to let me play guitar, another lad play bass, a music teacher play the harpsichord, on a Black Sabbath song called 'Fluff'. I think it's off *Sabbath Bloody Sabbath*, an instrumental thing. I remember I was literally shaking when I went on, even though it was just a bunch of parents. That was my only public performance before the Pistols' gig, so that's what I was expecting myself to experience. But weirdly enough, I didn't. I wasn't particularly nerve-wracking at all. I just went and got on with it.

DAWN BRADBURY: I couldn't make my mind up about Buzzcocks – but I loved Slaughter. I gelled with them more because they were a bit more rocky. Buzzcocks were a bit more *avant garde-y*. More poetic.

GLEN MATLOCK: It was quite an eye-opener to find that there was a scene somewhere other than the capital. I know that sounds a bit arrogant, but we just didn't know any better. The second gig was jumping, jumping. We premiered 'Anarchy In The UK' ... I think. Sorry, my chronological brain is a bit mixed up, for a variety of reasons.

PETE SHELLEY: I think that was the night they did 'Anarchy'. It was just like ... Yeah, that's a single.

The Sex Pistols did, indeed, play their new song, 'Anarchy In The UK', for the very first time that night. They were live-performance veterans by this stage but, for the first band due on stage before a packed Lesser Free Trade Hall, this was big stuff. But the Buzzcocks' guitarist, Pete Shelley, had come prepared. The college kid had a cunning plan to upstage Slaughter And The Dogs. He'd bought a super-cheap guitar from Woolworths just prior to the gig – he'd already sawn part of the guitar off and he had no intention of the instrument surviving the Buzzcocks' set intact.

HOWARD BATES: When we first got there, Pete Shelley was having real problems with his guitar. He'd chopped the top of his guitar off, like someone had hit it with an axe. The top was completely missing and he couldn't get it working and he was panicking. Spider, our guitarist, was a hippie, techie guy who knew how to take guitars apart and how to put them back together again. He said, 'Don't worry, I'll sort it out.' He got some silver foil from a fag packet, took the guitar apart, found the connection, whacked a bit of silver paper round it and got Shelley's guitar working.

PETE SHELLEY: We didn't really have time to be nervous. I mean, being nervous is a luxury when you've got time to think. I just remember Malcolm saying, 'If Buzzcocks aren't on in five minutes, they're not going on.' So we just had to get ready and on we go. The worst thing to do is to show the audience fear, because they can smell it. And when they know that you're nervous, that gets them nervous – and they don't like that. So if you can just go on and shout at them and play the music and get off, they think, 'Wow, that's amazing'. I was wearing ridiculously tight salmon-pink jeans and a shirt which I had made myself, dark glasses, pumps ... and I just ended up smashing the guitar to pieces. Which was good fun and lots of noise. We didn't get lynched. It was really all about seeing what you could get away with. It's remarkable how much you can get away with before people say, 'Stop! Stop!' I'm still waiting for them to say 'stop'.

HOWARD DEVOTO: People clapped! Did we do an encore? I doubt it. I should think we planned not to do an encore but to have our spectacular ending, where we all disappeared off separate bits of the stage and have a bit of a tussle with Peter's guitar. We were out there for twenty minutes and we got away with it and people clapped and we were in the music papers the following week.

PETE SHELLEY: Totally chaotic. I mean, we all had a vague idea of what we were supposed to be doing so we had to make everything else up. I remember there being two long thin dressing rooms, but we didn't have all that much dressing to do. We just went on and went off and packed up and got ready to watch the Sex Pistols. It was a case of just getting the gig and going, 'One, two, three, four!' and all finishing at the same time.

HOWARD DEVOTO: I seem to remember there being a Slaughter And The Dogs contingent there, because I certainly made a few disparaging remarks about them and there was some kind of hissing going on out there in the auditorium.

MARK E. SMITH: I remember thinking … 'We could do better than that'. The one thing Buzzcocks did do was break things down.

PETE SHELLEY: Things like this didn't happen in Manchester – it was easy to contemplate spending a life of being completely unknown.

GLEN MATLOCK: Buzzcocks played – I think it was their first gig. They had a guitar that was only half a guitar. He didn't like the top half and just cut it off with a saw. I dug the way that, when they finished their set – they finished up with 'Boredom' – there was an interminable guitar solo and Devoto just went up to Shelley and pulled his lead out. That was a good end to the set.

JOHN MAHER: Howard had this thing with Pete Shelley. He'd said, 'What we'll do is, on the last song, I'm going to try to take your guitar off you. We'll get in a struggle and I'll rip the strings off.' Then they said to me, 'Jump off the stage and run out the back door as if you're leaving the building.' And sure enough, I did. As soon as we'd finished, I was off. I ran down the back and went down the stairs. Then I thought, 'Shit... what do I do now? I've got to go back and get my gear'. So I got in the lift and there was a guy in there with really long hair. He was going, 'Wow, you guys were really brilliant!' It was Paul Morley. I think he must have had a haircut the next day.

HOWARD BATES: I had the longest hair on stage but Paul Morley had the longest hair in the audience. He had longer hair than me. After the gig, we got it cut.

PETE SHELLEY: The whole basic premise of the band in the first place was so ridiculous and laughable, we were enjoying every moment of it, it was completely the wrong thing to do. We started doing the most uncommercial form of music you could possibly imagine and not even bother to play it very well. So as a result of that, we didn't let our lack of experience stand in the way of having a go – it was perfect. Every day there was amazement over why we hadn't been arrested.

JOHN MAHER: We hadn't been playing together that long. We hadn't played on a stage before. Sound checks? Onstage sound? How's it sounding through the monitors? There was none of that. It was being thrown it at the deep end: get on, get the job done. We didn't analyse it in any depth beforehand. Howard possibly did. He was much older than me. He was eight or nine years older and it was his idea to get the band together in the first place. Something had sparked off in Howard to go and

Above left: Mike Day and Wayne Barrett of Slaughter and the Dogs (presumably before the barrage of peanuts). © *Peter Oldham*

Above right: Keyboard player Dave 'Zok' Howard of Solstice ('Bolton's Third Biggest Rock Band') wildly missing the point of Sex Pistols: 'We'd played and we'd gone down alright. Then this lot came on and they were bloody crap'.

© *Dave Howard*

Below: Dressed in tattered rags and boiler suits, and with hair measurable inches shorter than anyone else in the room, the Sex Pistols take the stage and change the course of rock music. © *Paul Welsh*

Above: A shot from the first gig captures the sparsity of the audience that turned up to witness the Pistols that night. Many would go on to form their own influential bands...
© *Paul Welsh*

Below: ...For instance Steve Diggle, Howard Devoto and Pete Shelley (left to right), who were up and running as Buzzcocks in time to open for the second Lesser Free Trade Hall gig.
© *Peter Oldham*

Above: The second gig. Their live stage presence was 'intimidation on legs', in the words of audience member Peter Oldham.

© *Peter Oldham*

Below left: 'Steve Jones, pulling a furious guitar pose as a rather bemused long-hair in a velvet jacket gazes into the distance to locate the bar.'

© *Peter Oldham*

Below right: Note the ever decreasing structural integrity of Johnny Rotten's shirt as the gig progresses.

© *Paul Burgess Archive*

Above left: Johnny Rotten showcasing his 'really, really long, long stare' live on Tony Wilson's *So It Goes*.

Above right: *So It Goes* presenter and soon-to-be Factory Records founder Tony Wilson – the only one with any idea what was about to be unleashed on the audience.

Below: Johnny Rotten projects pure, corrosive fury into British living rooms and somewhere a producer cringes as Jordan (complete with swastika armband) manages to flail into shot (right).

© *Granada Television*

seek out the Sex Pistols and come back to Manchester and set up the gig. He was obviously very enthused by them. He was on a mission; I was just a young kid that got roped in. I didn't really have any understanding of what was going on. I was just there and did my bit. I wasn't a mover and shaker, I just did my bit and went along for the ride.

STEVE SHY: I got what was happening when Buzzcocks came on. That did it for me. I thought, 'I'm going to remember this for the rest of my life.'

Up next: Slaughter And The Dogs. Wayne Barrett appears to wear a backless blouse and has a wedge haircut. Mick Rossi sports a fringed jumpsuit and a hairdo seemingly modelled on Dave Hill from Slade.

STEVE SHY: Wayne was wearing a satin bib and braces that night. When you saw what Pete and Howard were wearing, it didn't fit.

HOWARD BATES: It was a proper venue, a proper theatre, rather than the back of a pub with beer crates stuck together to make a stage. I think we probably played averagely. We mainly had covers and a handful of our own songs. I can remember being on stage and feeling nervous as hell. It was rammed. I think we played OK. Don't forget, we were young kids. It was a massive thing. A lot of bands at the time – even the Pistols and Buzzcocks – were four or five years older, which was a massive chasm in musical education. It was very tense before. There was a lot of energy about the place. When we came on, we didn't go down fantastically well with everyone. We had our own partisan contingent, then these other people who didn't know what the fuck was going on. It was a bit of a cauldron.

HOWARD DEVOTO: If there was trouble, I don't really know about it. I know that the Lesser Free Trade Hall wasn't prepared to take any more bookings afterwards. Whether that was down to something innocent, like a bit of graffiti in the gents or something like that, I've no idea. But they certainly weren't anxious to accept any more bookings. I can't even think why.

PAUL MORLEY: Slaughter And The Dogs were a joke band to me at the time. One of my great claims to fame that no one knows, because it was all so early and ridiculous, is that I actually almost got thrown out of that second show. For some bizarre reason I was flinging peanuts at Wayne Barrett, the singer of Slaughter And The Dogs. I had no idea of what being punk was and I don't think it was even called punk then, but it seemed important for me to make a statement – and my early statement, my first ever punk statement, was flinging peanuts at Wayne Barrett, because I thought he looked like a really dodgy copy of Bryan Ferry. Flicking peanuts and shouting. He tried to get me thrown out. I didn't like Slaughter And The Dogs. But now, in hindsight, they are probably one of the great lost representatives of a true working-class punk spirit.

PETE SHELLEY: I remember somebody losing a wallet and I went up and, without the aid of any amplification, shouted at everybody to be quiet, then announced a wallet had been found. It's all part of the public spiritedness.

PAUL MORLEY: I've never ever been a hooligan in my life, I'd never been naughty at school and suddenly, faced with Wayne Barrett's hair, I just had to throw something at him to say, 'You are inauthentic!' And I did.

PETER HOOK: A coach-load of Cockneys came down and it started going off in a big fight between the Cockneys and the Mancs, for some unknown reason. It just got really heavy. Buzzcocks set actually went OK, there was no trouble but, when the Sex Pistols came on, it all kicked off.

PAUL WELSH: It was exciting – at first John Lydon was saying, 'You're like a bunch of statues,' and, 'You'll get piles in your backsides sitting there like that.' By the end they did 'No Fun' and Lydon smiled and said, 'You're lots of fun really.' We weren't expecting that.

STEVE SHY: When Rotten came on. Bang. You ducked down in your seat, because you thought he was staring at you. Everyone in the place thought they were being stared at. He had that control. He should have been a drag artist, he has such sarcasm. Just like the answers you get off drag queens when someone slags them off. He was that quick.

VANESSA CORLEY: It was rubbish. When the Pistols came on, half the audience started spitting and half the audience started retaliating. At the time I probably thought, 'What a waste of money – I'd rather be somewhere else.'

LORRAINE JOYCE: It didn't last very long. They started throwing chairs and everything. I think that was the friends who they'd brought with them. It was just sort of set up.

EDDIE GARRITY: There were fights breaking out all the time. There was a big security team down there from Wythenshawe – maybe they started most of the fights. If it wasn't going to kick off, they'd probably been told to start trouble, with there being a lot of press down there, you know, get some publicity going.

STEVE SHY: There was a lot of trouble. I'm sat there with my cousin – her first and only punk gig – and she was hiding between my legs. Someone had thrown a pint pot and the glass had come raining down. It was kicking off.

PETER HOOK: It went off on the big night and then Paul Morley was trying to get everybody going. 'Come on, Mancs! Come on … let's get the Cockneys!' All running round. It was amazing.

PAUL MORLEY: I got very overexcited, like a hyperactive child.

PAUL WELSH: People have said that these people came up from London antagonising the locals. I didn't see that. I saw kids from Wythenshawe who'd come to see Slaughter And The Dogs. They were coming up to people and saying, 'Are you Wythie or are you Manc?' If you said Manc, they'd hit you. I didn't really see a lot of violence. I'd been to the Free Trade Hall when Lou Reed played and the front five rows were destroyed and the roadies were hitting people in the face with mic stands. Nothing like that going on.

PETER HOOK: I remember Mick Rossi was there. He was like the one leading it all; leading the charges across the Lesser Free Trade Hall. Strange thing now is that I went back to a concert there and the room seemed so small. It's like going back to school and seeing your assembly. When you go back, it's tiny.

PETER OLDHAM: Buzzcocks and Slaughter And The Dogs were having a scrap at the side of the stage. It was like an Eric Morecambe thing [holds himself by the throat]: the curtain kept flicking and somebody kept dashing back on the other side.

EDDIE GARRITY: I was backstage, looking after the beer, so I was tucking into that. Then I thought I'd better go and look at this band, the Pistols. I went to the side of the stage and just stuck my head out and a bottle went 'ping', right on my head.

HOWARD BATES: Eddie Garrity came as a mate and ended up roadieing. He got bottled and had blood running down his face. It wasn't a kids' party atmosphere, that's for sure.

EDDIE GARRITY: I remember the Pistols came off and they were like pretty concerned, because all blood was running down my face. Johnny said to me, 'You want to go off to hospital with that.' I said, 'No ... I'll just have another beer.' All the lads were coming in, so I didn't want to seem soft. I'm there with blood pouring down my head, my mate Pete had been punched on the nose. Someone says, 'You're a right bloody mob, aren't you? Headbanger here and him with a nose bleed.' And the name sort of came about, that night.

There are several fascinating visual records of the 20 July gig. One is the 8mm cine film shot by Mark Roberts, the college friend of Devoto's, who had also shot film of the first gig and of Howard being arty at Lower Broughton Road. It features all three bands but the majority of the time is given over to the Sex Pistols. Slaughter And The Dogs can be seen large-ing it around the stage in their blouses, having quite the most fantastic time. Pete Shelley is, indeed, wearing ridiculously tight salmon-pink jeans and sunglasses. Johnny Rotten is sporting a silver belt and a skinny black tie and, at one point, rips his shirt off. Steve Jones is wearing a Vivienne Westwood top with zips on and is using his trademark white Gibson Les Paul guitar, with 1950s-style pin-up girls stuck to it. The audience's dress sense is a little snappier than last time too.

HOWARD DEVOTO: I think Mark shot three reels. We decided, OK, we'll have one reel of us and then save two for the Pistols. I don't even know if they knew they were being filmed. Maybe we'd have said, 'Do you mind if we film?' ... I've no idea actually.

PETE SHELLEY: It's like our copy of the Zupruder tapes [footage of the Kennedy assassination] – instead of the grassy knoll, you can see Howard lurking onstage. It's like seeing Charlie Chaplin ... jerky pictures of yourself.

HOWARD DEVOTO: It's curious because, for a start, there's no sound. It's like seeing silent-movie footage or something, but I think, for somebody who hadn't handled a movie camera before, Mark actually did a very good job with it.

Another record is a set of still photographs taken by student Peter Oldham. My favourite is the shot of Steve Jones pulling a furious guitar pose as a rather bemused long-hair in a velvet jacket looks into the distance to locate the bar. Oldham had also been to the first gig and afterwards had made a note that, if the band returned, he'd 'take a few snaps'.

PETER OLDHAM: I thought, 'I'll get some pictures of that', more for my own amusement than anything, you know. For one thing, you weren't going to take your best camera down there just in case somebody ripped it out of your hands or it got confiscated, so it was a matter of just popping up out of your seat with your Zenith and flashing a few pictures. I'm a much better photographer now. I'm glad I took the photographs in as much as they're a record of the event more than anything.

Because it's all 'kicking off' in the hall, the Sex Pistols set is shorter than last time and they make a hasty exit. The time had come for the most important part of the evening. Counting the cash.

HOWARD DEVOTO: Malcolm has his hand fairly firmly on the tiller of the money boat. We weren't doing it for the money. We were doing it just to play our gig. Maybe we got slipped ten quid for getting to the end of our set.

PETE SHELLEY: All the proceeds went with Malcolm. We got ten pounds as our fee. I don't know what happened to the rest of the money. He spent it on the Sex Pistols. You could live like a king for ten pounds. More than a whole week's dole money.

MICK ROSSI: They were upstairs, counting the money. Malcolm's going, one for you, one for me...

WAYNE BARRETT: ...one up the trouser leg and all the rest of it. I think he must have screwed us for round about a hundred and fifty quid, something like that...

MICK ROSSI: Allegedly...

WAYNE BARRETT: ...allegedly.

PETER OLDHAM: I nearly ran them over on Oxford Road, the Sex Pistols, on the way to the second gig. They were going across for a burger or something. Could have changed musical history really, couldn't I?

MICK ROSSI: The aim after the Free Trade Hall thing was then for us to try to hit London and we had a few false starts but we finally got there. That was the next step. Then records. Because we started to realise then what was going on.

WAYNE BARRETT: Malcolm suggested to go down and to try to play in The Roxy, and centre around that area, so we went down to London. We did tidy our look up before going down there.

MICK ROSSI: No more irons basically.

WAYNE BARRETT: No more irons, no more satin and things like that. The brown thing I was wearing at the Free Trade Hall, I think it was my mum who made that.

HOWARD BATES: Spider, our guitarist, wasn't liking what we were doing. The Pistols' gig was his last gig with us. He went downstairs, his mum and dad came to pick him up in a little Ford Anglia and, musically, that's the last we saw of him.

STEVE DIGGLE: In a way, the second gig was more important. The first time was like a rehearsal, no one really saw the first one. In terms of the people in the room, the second one was where the world got to know about it. From that little gig at that place in Manchester, it went to America and all around the world.

PAUL MORLEY: I saw the Sex Pistols a dozen times and for me it was the equivalent of seeing Elvis Presley 'cause it was always fantastic. It was always the most remarkable kind of show. It was like extreme show business. It was real show business ... they were entertainers, they weren't sloppy or anything, they put their heart and soul into it and they really worked hard. At that second show, you just got the feeling that something really important had happened.

STEVE SHY: I was ripping my T-shirt during the gig. I fell in love with Lydon. It was pure love. Lust! I thought,

'That's the person I'd like to be'. It's only ever happened with him, [footballer Eric] Cantona and Mark E. Smith. They are their own people – they don't give a shit what people think about them.

JON THE POSTMAN: You knew what they were going to be like so ... that sort of expectation wasn't there anymore but they were still as good at that second gig. I saw them a third time in December of that year, at The Electric Circus on the 'Anarchy' tour, and they'd lost it already by then ... they sounded quite weak.

PAUL WELSH: The second time I went to see the Sex Pistols, all the rough edges had been smoothed. I didn't like them. They were too musical, they'd improved so much in the space of six weeks. That initial performance was the best I ever saw them play. I was expecting the same sort of thing – we weren't expecting the way they'd improved. They were more slick. On the second night, Buzzcocks impressed me more than anyone else. They were like the Sex Pistols were like at the first show.

Paul Welsh again wrote up his thoughts for the next edition of his *Penetration* magazine: 'Local punks Buzzcocks coming over as a cross between Ramones and Sex Pistols, supported admirably, creating havoc and chaos onstage,' he wrote. Welsh was less kind about Slaughter And The Dogs, describing them as, 'juvenile pooftahs. Perhaps their parents could do us all a favour and keep them indoors at nightime.' As for the Pistols: 'How can a bunch of musical incompetents write stuff like this then? They have got talent and it's surfacing fast.'

PAUL WELSH: After the second gig, I got Malcolm McLaren's phone number and I rang him up. I'd read about the punk festival at the 100 Club in London [on 20–21 September 1976] and thought we could do the same thing in Manchester. Malcolm gave me the phone numbers of all the people involved – he said the Pistols would do it. I rang The Damned and they said they'd do it ... Siouxsie And The Banshees, Subway Sect. When I rang The Clash, I spoke to their manager Bernie Rhodes and all they kept going on about was me being a capitalist and that they didn't want to line the pockets of people like me. I was penniless at the time. Malcolm then asked me if I'd like to promote the upcoming Anarchy Tour – Ramones, Heartbreakers, Pistols, Clash and The Damned. The Ramones later pulled out. I didn't have the thousand pounds he wanted so he asked if I could find them somewhere to play. I rang the Free Trade Hall and I asked if they could play there. They said OK but we'd have to pay something up front in case of broken seats. We booked it and I told Malcolm. A week later the ad appeared in the music press with all the dates then, a week after that, the ad reappeared with all the dates crossed out. The Pistols were banned from everywhere. And that was that.

In fact, Manchester was one of the few places the Pistols did play during the ill-fated Anarchy Tour of December 1976. They played twice at the dungeon-like Electric Circus in Collyhurst, a former prog and heavy-rock club. Thrown into the public spotlight after they were goaded into swearing by former Granada journalist and presenter Bill Grundy, the Pistols were now front-page news and Public Enemy Number One – venues up and down the land pulled the plug on them but Manchester still laid on a warm welcome. But things had changed.

PAUL WELSH: At The Electric Circus it was getting a bit ordinary by that stage. The Pistols were still good. I wasn't disappointed. But it wasn't the same as the first gig.

PETER HOOK: I remember going to The Electric Circus to see the Pistols. That was when the punk thing had kicked off and everybody hated punks. I remember all the punters queuing up the road and the kids in Collyhurst had broken all these railings off and they were on the top of these flats, throwing the rails at the punks like javelins. Unbelievable – the reaction of normal people against punks. We met Ian Curtis for the first time at The Electric Circus. He had a green military jacket on with the word 'hate' on the back in white letters, which I thought was fantastic. 'Hate'. Incredible.

The Pistols' gig at The Electric Circus on 19 December marked the end of the band's visits to Manchester. They wouldn't return to the city to play live for 31 years and that would be to play to 15,000 people at the Manchester Arena. Their 1976 gigs at the Circus – and especially the Lesser Free Trade Hall – left the city energised and jolted into action. There already seemed to be a hierarchy in place too: *I saw the Pistols at The Circus... well I saw them in July at the Lesser Free Trade Hall... that's nothing, I saw them at the first gig on 4 June. You never... I swear!*

PETE SHELLEY: There's a lot of unanswered questions about those gigs – might have been something in the beer...

The confusion in people's minds over the two Sex Pistols gigs at the Lesser Free Trade Hall will probably never be fully separated. Too much time and too many mind-altering liquids and substances have passed through most of those at the gigs by now. It's probably true to say that, although the second gig was nowhere near as shocking on the evidence of those present, it was more of an event. The concert on 20 July 1976 probably did more than the first to change the world over the next forty years. More people were physically there to spread the word, to form bands, to start writing for the music press and to get their flared trousers taken in. Sharpish.

Not that anyone's suggesting that any kind of plan was unfolding here but wouldn't it be great if we could involve everybody else of a like mind who hadn't been able to get to the Lesser Free Trade Hall in June and July? What if the Pistols could get on TV and into people's homes? Then it could all *really* kick off.

SO IT GOES › SO IT GOES ›
SO IT GOES › ›SO IT GOES › ›SO IT GOES

Mr Anthony Wilson requests the
pleasure of your company, and whatever
attention you care to bring to an
intimate musical evening
Wednesday 25th August 1976 6.40pm
Granada Television
Quay Street Manchester 3

A ticket for the first Sex Pistols television appearance, on *So It
Goes* with Tony Wilson. The TV audience – and, indeed, the
show's producers – had no idea what was to follow.

CHAPTER SIX

EVEN BETTER THAN THE LOVELY JONI MITCHELL

The Sex Pistols' appearance on local television on 1 December 1976 sealed their national notoriety. The 'filth and the fury' that was broadcast on Thames Television's *Today* programme consisted of Rotten saying 'shit' twice – very quietly – and guitarist Steve Jones calling host Bill Grundy a 'dirty bastard', a 'dirty fucker' and a 'fucking rotter'. This was, quite possibly, the last ever recorded use of the word 'rotter' in mainland Britain. Very few people even saw the item, as the *Today* show was only broadcast in the London area. Because it made the front pages of the tabloid press the following day, many people assume this was the Pistols' first television appearance. It wasn't. The first time the Sex Pistols appeared on British television was on *So It Goes*, recorded at Granada Television in Manchester three months earlier.

The programme was presented by Tony Wilson, abetted by Australian 'cultural commentator' Clive James and, occasionally, by satirist Peter Cook.

It was what used to be called a 'soft network' show: shown in more than one region but not across the country as a whole. It was a very odd programme indeed. But events leading up to the show were even stranger. *Carry On Swastika*, if you will. It's amazing it was ever broadcast but broadcast it was – albeit in a slightly doctored form.

TONY WILSON (presenter – *So It Goes*): In late 1975/ early 1976, my friends and I here at Granada were preparing to turn our regional *What's On* programme into a late-night music show. And we were turning it into a comedy show, with Clive James doing comedy sketches, because there was, in our opinion, no music worth covering.

CHRIS PYE (producer – *So It Goes*): It was a proper TV show, you understand. It was just because of the people we were dealing with ... it got a little bit sort of edgy sometimes. But it was a normal schedule; we had a studio and cameramen, the sound guys turned up and the floor manager wore the headphones. It was all quite normal. Until the Sex Pistols turned up.

PETER WALKER (director – *So It Goes*): I worked for Granada for twenty one years. I started out on sound and then eventually became a dubbing mixer and then a director, but I had a hankering to do music. I became involved in lots of kids shows, The Arrows, the Bay City Rollers and eventually this programme called *So It Goes*. I was the automatic choice to be the director because there wasn't anybody else around at the time to do that sort of show. Chris Pye – and myself to a lesser extent – didn't really didn't want them [the Sex Pistols] on the programme. They'd been in Tony Wilson's mind right from the word go. Every pre-production meeting we'd have about who was going to be on that week's show, he would say, 'When are we going to get the Sex Pistols on?' 'Oh, Tony, belt up, you can't have them on, they're not musical, they're not musicians, they're just layabouts.' I think Chris finally relented under pressure and said, 'OK ... they're on the last show.'

TONY WILSON: It was on the last show of the first series that one was able to infiltrate ... it was really a question of getting the Pistols on. The entire British press – with the exception of *The Times* and the *Daily Mail* – hated *So It Goes*. And I mean *hated* it. In fact, we were responsible for a great resurgence of love for *The Old Grey Whistle Test*, because these disgraceful people on *So It Goes* were not treating music with the respect it deserved.

GORDON BURNS (Granada TV Presenter): A lot of us were thinking, 'How can we let this go on air? All these horrible, nasty groups spitting and swearing?' Sex Pistols and all that lot? At the time it was heavy stuff. A lot of people were saying that these guys shouldn't be allowed in the building and that it was disgraceful and, 'What's Tony doing?' But that was one of Granada's strengths – they backed him. Tony had the vision that we never had and it was another milestone in pop music.

PETER WALKER: Before the Sex Pistols turned up, the programme was very much Chris Pye's baby. He was the instigator behind the whole series. He was very much influenced by bands like the Eagles and the East Coast, cool, laid-back, American sound, and absolutely besotted by Eric Clapton. He [Pye] was a bit of a guitarist himself. He just couldn't understand why he should put on a band who couldn't really play that well and were more into three or four chords ... at the most.

CHRIS PYE: We had Clive James on every show doing a monologue. We had a guy called Steve who came on and reviewed films he'd never seen. We said to him, 'What do you make of this week's movie?' He'd never seen the movie, but he talked fluently for about a minute and a half. It wasn't a magazine show; it was like a kind of bits-and-pieces show.

PETER WALKER: The show for Tony was a different proposition. He wanted to have a lot of exposure. He was very much an egocentric sort of presenter, very much involved in what the programme looked like, how he wanted it to be, and the music, perhaps at that stage, was secondary to his own career.

PAUL MORLEY: Tony Wilson had a weird energy and a fantastic ability to persuade the powers-that-be. It was ridiculous to be able to get a music show on television. Unbelievable. But that's what was fantastic about it. Tony Wilson in the North West in 1976, 1977, 1978 was like John Stapleton [*GMTV*] or Richard Madeley [*Richard And Judy/ This Morning*]. It kind of looked like that. Tony, as much as he was on it very quickly, was always one step behind. He still had the long hair and the flares and the leather blouson jacket. Clearly an interesting show that put on the best new music, but it was presented by the most peculiar character and got lacerating reviews from London. They couldn't understand why suddenly this very square-looking bloke was presenting this hip show. Also, what was fascinating about it was that Tony Wilson's sidekick was Clive James, who presented this kind of weird little essay on pop culture.

TONY WILSON: We'd enjoy making jokes. We'd have Clive James being Demis Roussos or we'd have Peter Cook talking about his obscene [*Derek And Clive*] album of that period. So we did a comedy show, with these rather ordinary bands. The pub-rock bands, I wouldn't have anything to do with. But then again, they wouldn't have anything to do with a late-night TV show. It was just an awful period. All that crap on *Top Of The Pops*. As I point out to people, then, just like it is today, it looked exactly the same. People were exactly as badly dressed. There were one or two good pop songs, mostly it was drivel. Very similar to today.

All television programmes are, by their very nature and structure, stressful creatures. But *So It Goes* seems to have been specifically designed to be as difficult to make as possible.

CHRIS PYE: The whole thing was a bit fraught. You had to wait for Clive James to arrive, because he came by train. Some shows we had Peter Cook on, but we had to send somebody down to London to get him; we didn't want him to drink too much on the train. So that was all a bit dodgy.

PETER WALKER: The one big difference on that particular day was the Sex Pistols. Now we'd obviously heard about their career so far and we knew that they were ... not dangerous, shall we say, but unorthodox in the way that they presented themselves and the way they performed.

JORDAN: The combination of Peter Cook, Clive James and the Sex Pistols and all those weird, hippie bands, and Tony and that denim and clogs ... well, it's got to be a winner.

Indeed, a winner it was. What makes the Sex Pistols' performance on *So It Goes* even more remarkable is to see it in the context of the whole programme – with the comedy and with the performances of the other bands. They only get three minutes airtime at the end of a half-an-hour show but the Pistols stand out like the sorest of thumbs. The strange way the performance ends – and the way it was altered by Granada's technical staff – actually increases its power.

TONY WILSON: I don't think that I was that arrogant at that time to refuse to have bands in the studio. I wouldn't conceive having the Rick Wakemans and pub rock and that shit. I wasn't that arrogant ... but nevertheless I wouldn't have wanted to even bother with any of that shite. It was awful, awful. That was the last show of the series ... couldn't get any fucking bands at all. We decided that we'd have three unsigned bands, the Pistols being one of them. But the other ones, they were all crap.

JORDAN: Tony couldn't have been nicer. He was really, really charming and nice to the band and really calm about it. I would imagine he probably didn't know what was going to happen till it did happen. It was a very 'by the seat of your pants' sort of performance. Not even John [Rotten] would know what was going to happen 'til he did it.

PETER WALKER: Nobody, apart from perhaps Tony, had seen them [the Pistols] performing live. We did not know what we were going to be in for. I think there was a lot of angst in the studios about what they were going to do: are they going to start smashing up the place? Are they going to be like The Who? The Who, once upon a time, came in and they just destroyed the studio.

JORDAN: I think John [Rotten] was a bit nervy about it on the way up, because I remember the train journey. It was a bit of a worry but, once he got there, once he saw Tony Wilson with his jeans jacket and his clogs, we knew we'd made it. We just called him a bloody hippie when we walked in: 'My God! What do you think you look like, bloody hippie?' We didn't know what to expect – music companies were all full of hippies – but we didn't really expect Tony to be a hippie. We gave him such a hard time. I'm so sorry Tony, in retrospect.

To watch *So It Goes* today is something of a challenge. The title sequence is a series of shape-changing caterpillars and snails that evolve into a droog-like image of Tony Wilson, as if taken from *A Clockwork Orange*. Then Jordan pops up – dressed like a Nazi Myra Hyndley – and declares to camera that 'The Sex Pistols are, if possible, even better than the lovely Joni Mitchell.' So far, so baffling.

JORDAN: Tony Wilson asked me to get up and introduce the band and he said, 'You can say whatever you want really.' I think he thought I was just going to say, 'Here's the Sex Pistols.' But I didn't. I think it was something to do with the Bowles Brothers [who were also on the show]. There was an argument – involving John – and Joni Mitchell was mentioned. John made it up to get up their noses.

After Jordan's introduction, the music commences. The first band up play superbly but these boys are in the wrong place at the wrong time. Over the next thirty minutes – just as it had done for Solstice – the shape of rock music changes right underneath the platform-soled feet of the group known as Gentlemen. They are Be Bop Deluxe-style pomp-rockers from north Manchester. They whack out a tune called 'My Ego's Hurting Me'. They are super-complex, ultra-confident and they rhyme 'What a drag you are' with 'Jaguar'. At one point, the bass player and lead guitarist swap left hands and fret each other's instruments. One of their number sports flared and fringed leather trousers. After five minutes of highly proficient gesticulating, they finish. 'Nice one!' declares Wilson.

CHRIS PYE: Bloody hell, who are Gentlemen?

HOWARD KINGSTON (lead singer – Gentlemen): We were what you'd call a progressive band. We were into Yes, Genesis, that kind of thing. I was twenty three. We had to hire a hall near Manchester University to sort of audition for Wilson as we had no gigs coming up. He got us on the show. So he was OK by us. There was a feeling that he was an OK person, but also that he was out for himself. But I liked the way he managed to play the straight news guy for *Granada Reports*, then the music guy on *So It Goes*. He was good cop and bad cop.

PETER WALKER: I remember nothing about Gentlemen obviously, because who would have a crap name like Gentlemen? Don't know why we ever had them on. Gentlemen? Come on, do me a favour.

GLEN MATLOCK: Didn't realise there were any other bands on with us.

HOWARD DEVOTO: Wow, there were other bands? I would doubt that we would have sat through any other bands that were on – that would have been all part of the attitude.

The next band up are the Bowles Brothers. They lay down 'Charlie's Nuts', an acoustic, summery jazz number with a Manhattan Transfer vibe that includes plenty of 'skoodly-doodly-wah-wahs'.

JORDAN: It was truly bizarre: not just the other bands but the audience. They were just like ... they looked like prisoners waiting to die. They were just gone. They'd had it, brain dead, whole lot of them, hadn't got a clue. But then, if you look at the previous bands that were on the show, you can see why they'd been lulled into this sort of catatonic state. Diddlie diddlies and blinkin' split jeans and flared leather jackets. It was a madhouse. We were sitting in this dressing room, listening to this folk band with a double bass. We didn't know what we had let ourselves in for.

HOWARD KINGSTON: We had to share a green room with the Pistols. They were obnoxious – drinking, making a mess, disrespecting musicians we had a lot of respect for: Joni Mitchell, Steely Dan. In retrospect, I get it. I see that, although that was their shtick, music had gotten out of hand

and needed to change, but I didn't like it. We nearly got into a fight with them – Clive James advised us not to. In a way, I wish we had fought them – it would have been good publicity for us. They didn't like what we represented and we didn't like what they represented. There was an element that the show was all about the Pistols. They were the headliners after all.

Next, under the heading of 'Brain Damage', Clive James does a monologue directly to camera about music-press apathy.

HOWARD DEVOTO: Malcolm did invite Pete and I down to the *So It Goes* thingy. I guess they wanted as much support as they could. I've got very confused memories of that day. I seem to remember Clive James being on. There was an audience and Clive James was trying to kind of get this rapport going. Meanwhile, the Pistols were trying to sort of psyche themselves up to perform. There was definitely a fair bit of antagonism going on between the band and Clive James.

GLEN MATLOCK: Clive James thought, 'Well, I'm going to take Rotten on.' And Rotten just made mincemeat of him. Absolute mincemeat.

TONY WILSON: I remember the Pistols were extremely badly behaved all day. I remember them lying on the floor of the reception foyer here at Granada, which was quite funny and upset people. I remember Malcolm giving me a T-shirt – which I still have – of a teenage boy smoking. I remember Clive James in the green room getting very upset with them and having an argument with them and not liking them. That was the day – that moment – that Clive James grew old. Because Clive didn't get it. He still doesn't. He and Lydon [Johnny Rotten] had a real row and he hated that. It was all a bit chaotic.

JORDAN: Peter Cook was on: he was really cool, he was really great. He was sort of a bit drunk and a bit nervy. He thought the band were great; he really liked them. He threw me a packet of fags across the studio. And there was this bloke, Clive James. I think his life changed after that day; I think he was never the same man again. He was upset and he thought the band were in bad taste. John and I laid into him really badly and called him a baldie old Sheila at the top of our voices ... 'You baldie old Sheila!'

The only warning of things to come is a cleverly played-in clip of Jerry Lee Lewis, performing up close and dirty to a bunch of kids at the very same Granada TV studios. It's a performance that's worth a book in itself. Lewis, his sweat-bathed face covered by a hanging, curled fringe, is genuinely terrifying. His appearance is actually upsetting; it's an horrific and terrific piece of television. Coming out of the clip, Wilson points to it as containing 'energy so lacking in today's big bands – perhaps coke isn't the real thing.' Clive James then interviews Peter Cook about the *Derek And Clive Live* album. The satirist's hands are visibly shaking and he refers to Dudley Moore as a 'midget poof'. Cook gets a few laughs from the audience. Cook would have another involvement with punk, at its tail end. In 1978 he presented ATV's *Revolver* show. In this late-night shoutfest, he played the part of a reluctant club host, introducing punk/new-wave bands of the day, often with a stripper behind him. After The Only Ones/The Lurkers/Eater had played, he would invariably insult them, before bringing on the next group. Then the process would repeat itself. It was *so* punk rock.

PETER WALKER: All the rehearsals went fine. They went, 'Oh, they're nice enough, they're just, you know, a group of lads ... pleasant.' But when it came to transmission and they started to perform, that was just a total eye-opener. Nobody could believe it. There was so much energy coming out of that group, so much commitment. They saved that performance for when they knew the cameras were rolling.

JORDAN: I think the Pistols did quite a tame rehearsal in the afternoon, I'm not even sure if it was the same song; I think they sang something else. So it wasn't anything like the final product. The crew were led to believe it was going to be peachy and nice, but I mean they would have been stupid to think that. The thing about the Pistols is they did, to some extent, feed off other people's aggression. When the crowds just got so adoring, when the audience got so adoring, the Pistols weren't quite themselves anymore. You can see it in that shot of John at the end; he was feeding off the negativity that was coming from the crowd. In a way, he didn't really like people liking him because it meant that he wasn't doing it right.

GLEN MATLOCK: We were big 'eads! It was good that we got a break on the TV so more people could see us. I've always said the way we got it together, it's got a direct analogy with *The Blues Brothers* movie. They were going round, getting everybody out of jail: 'Hey, we've got to get a band together! We're on a mission from God!' We were on a mission to stir things up a little bit ... and get something happening. So getting a TV show was one more step up the ladder. We considered it our right ... 'cause we were those kind of guys.

CHRIS PYE: Before the Pistols came along, we tended to take bands that were not Top 20 bands. Tony led the music policy really, so we didn't very often have straight up-and-down bands. We had people who were just slightly off kilter. That's what the policy was. We booked the Pistols – we knew they were kind of out there somewhere – so we booked them. And they went off the scale. I knew nothing about them at all until they arrived – they were difficult, they were odd, they were not what you expect. But they were a great booking.

GLEN MATLOCK: I haven't seen it [*So It Goes*] for a long time. You always see the little clip and you don't see the whole show.

CHRIS PYE: During the afternoon, we were rehearsing the band and, eventually, we got a phone call from the sixth floor, which was the management floor. In Granada, you can view what's going on in all the studios by turning your TV set on – an internal service. Sydney Bernstein was the chairman of the company. He'd been skimming through the channels and came across the Sex Pistols in the studio rehearsing. One of the Sex Pistols' entourage [Jordan] was wearing a swastika armband. Sydney, for a man of his age and his generation and his background, was really, really upset by this. He thought it was absolutely outrageous that we should be transmitting somebody with a swastika armband on a Granada programme. He wasn't worried about their hair. He wasn't worried about the fact they were aggressive. He just thought the swastika was really in bad taste. So he called down to me and said, 'This can't go out.' So it was my task to try to persuade the Sex Pistols that it was a jolly good idea to take off the swastika armband. The issue occupied about three hours.

JORDAN: Somebody noticed that I was wearing a shirt with a swastika armband and there was a real big do about it. I got taken in secrecy through this labyrinth of sets and corridors into wardrobe. There was a lot of gnashing of teeth and sucking of lips. And me, sort of standing my ground really, I said, 'That's the shirt, that's the way it should be, it's sewn on, I'm not taking it off, I'm not taking the shirt off.' Everyone got involved and there was a big do over it.

PETER WALKER: Our head of Granada TV at the time was Sydney Bernstein, who didn't actually like the Germans. We weren't allowed to have German microphones on the station. I was under very strict instructions not to show her or her armband in shot. But, of course, the Sex Pistols were very adamant that she had to be there, because she was part of their act.

JORDAN: I didn't know what had caused it. I just knew somebody must have spotted it. Firstly, I didn't think anything of it. Secondly, I thought, 'If somebody did notice it, I'd get away with it. I really was a bit bemused by it all.'

CHRIS PYE: I met Malcolm McLaren, because we had to talk to him about a couple of problems we had between the rehearsal and the show. I didn't know how to handle these guys; I didn't know how best to talk to them. So Malcolm was around and he was the intermediary between the TV studio and people like me and the band.

TONY WILSON: It's hard to remember the Nazi chic of punk. In the early days of the Pistols, anything Nazi was a way of shock, outrage, or whatever. On that particular afternoon, Jordan had a swastika armband on. I had to go and tell her, 'Listen, sorry love...' So if you look at the video, she has gaffer tape over the swastika armband. It was a wild day and unruly. They caused lots of trouble. Thank God.

CHRIS PYE: I think Tony spoke to the band because Tony was that kind of guy. Tony, he'll speak to anybody. I was more involved with trying to keep things calm. I was on 'keeping things calm' mode that day. I think Tony thought the band were great. I think he loved them. I've no idea what they made of him. They had a bit of a falling out. I think that they thought that Tony was some kind of ageing, naff person, because he was a TV presenter and he had really quite nice hair. I think they thought he was perhaps from a different generation.

TONY WILSON: I was a hippie, I was! I mean, if you look at me on *So It Goes*, introducing the Sex Pistols...

CHRIS PYE: I worked out that, if I went to talk to them – I was an even naffer person than Tony Wilson – they wouldn't be responding to me. So I said to Malcolm, 'This is not something that I think is the right thing. It will offend people and it's a big audience. I know you want to be an offensive band, an aggressive band, but it would be really helpful if you could take the armband off.' He went away into some room and, eventually, the armband had not come off, but the swastika itself had been covered up. A sufficient compromise.

JORDAN: Some bright spark came up with the idea that they would stick a piece of white tape over it – which I didn't want, Malcolm didn't want. There was another argument and in the end it came down to either you don't go on the show or you have it censored. Which it was. It looks kind of good being censored, because people think it's even more powerful, probably because they tried to stop me showing it. Some years later, after that incident with Clive, he wrote an article in the *Observer* and he was still banging on about it. He was really so seriously affronted and yet it was just commonplace to us. He was on a TV programme and he brought it up again; he brought up the incident with me and the shirt again 'cause it offended him so badly.

The Sex Pistols are not long on vocabulary but they make it for it by being short on temper. They attacked everything around them and had difficulty in being polite even to each other. Their leader, a foul-mouthed ball of acne called Kenny Frightful kept trying to kick himself in the stomach. My evening with the Sex Pistols left me feeling sad and old. This was what the pop dream had finally come to.

Clive James, the *Observer* – November 1976.

PAUL WELSH: That's when they started to try to outrage people. And be punks. At the first gig in Manchester, punk didn't exist. Within a few weeks, the fashion started to come in. They had the swastikas and all that. You could tell it was being done for a reason.

GLEN MATLOCK: They wanted us to do one number and we wanted to do two. And originally Tony Wilson had just wanted to interview John [Rotten]. John didn't really want to. I think he was a bit cagey about it. We didn't want him to do that, 'cause it was like, 'Ooh, he's getting more attention than us!' They compromised and said, 'Well, you can do two, but we'll only record one.' It was on a Sunday night and it was running really late and the cameramen were going to get triple time or whatever it was if it went over the witching hour. I broke a string in the first number and didn't have a spare guitar. So somebody had to go all the way to the dressing rooms that were on the other side of the studio, bring the string back and I laboriously put it on. Tony Wilson was trying to chat to Rotten. You know, 'Why wouldn't you come and talk to me? Are you afraid to talk to us?' I just piped up, 'No, it's because you're a cunt.' All the audience laughed.

TONY WILSON: If Glen was rude to me, that's a bit of a surprise, because Glen was the nice one. Great musicians are meant to be rude to tossers from the media. No problem with that.

CHRIS PYE: We rehearsed with them and they were not like anything I'd ever seen before. They were loud and brash and violent and, in my view, unmusical. And completely uncooperative. They were just weird. I'd never seen people like this before. They were just a ... *thing*. A fully formed live force. And it was difficult.

JORDAN: Soon as they [the audience] saw the Pistols come on – if you look at the footage of it – John's just like staring at them, daring 'em, you know? Drop dead!

[laughing] And they didn't move ... the whole gig! ... they didn't move at all. Just stood there ... just sat there.

Wilson delivers a link to camera, referring back to the Clive James/Peter Cook chat, stating that the *Derek And Clive* album has a warning on it. 'Our final live band tonight also have a warning on them. One of the most reviewed and reviled phenomenon of recent weeks – Sex Pistols...'

TONY WILSON: Either Matlock or Jones hits the guitar and you get this noise. I'm looking like this dumb ex-hippie – which, of course, I am – in my denims. And you get the noise. Then you get, I think, Lydon [Rotten] screaming, 'Woodstock ... coming to get yer!' Then they hit it. And it was stunning.

Rotten advises the audience to 'Get off your arse!' and the band, dressed in a mish-mash of King's Road clobber, homemade gear and brothel creepers, play 'Anarchy In The UK', the song they'd played live for the first time at the Lesser Free Trade Hall on 20 July.

Whatever your opinion of the Sex Pistols and their music, it is an extraordinary performance. Rotten sings his guts out. Steve Jones – who appears to have put on about three stone in weight since the Pistols' first Lesser Free Trade Hall gig three months earlier – chugs at his guitar, making flangey noises with guitar-effects pedals. Matlock harmonises with Rotten in a Karl Marx shirt. Cook is rapt with concentration. Jordan, her swastika covered with tape, throws a plastic chair during the middle eight.

DAWN BRADBURY: Have you seen it recently? It's so tame. It makes me laugh.

PETER WALKER: Because it was the first TV they'd ever done, they were just giving everything they could possibly give it, to make their point. Watching the pictures on the monitors was just amazing. The energy was reflected back from them, to me and back to them again. It was something new. It was totally different but it wasn't a breath of fresh air at all. You had underlying foulness in the air if you like. It caught on to an undertone; a feeling within the country.

PETE SHELLEY: The *So It Goes* broadcast at Granada ... both me and Howard went down. On one copy of the film, you actually see me and Howard on the opening shot. On another copy, you don't see us at all. We've been edited out of history.

PAUL MORLEY: You can see their entourage. You can see Shelley and Devoto in the audience and get a little hint of what it was like before the hype and the tabloid nonsense got hold of it. As an artistic kind of liberation. It was those early months that were important and it was great that *So It Goes* was around to trap it; to capture it.

HOWARD DEVOTO: I don't think we saw the whole programme. We probably hung out a bit with them [Sex Pistols] and turned up. We were there for their slot. I remember them being very effective. I also remember

Jordan's not entirely successful attempts to try to get a bit of trouble going down at the front of the stage by knocking a plastic chair over. But yeah, they were great on it.

JORDAN: I actually really wanted to just throw the chair at the audience, but it's not on really. They wouldn't have noticed if they got hit in the face anyway. It nearly hit Steve Jones, I think, and he has to kick it out of the way. I was doing what we'd normally do at a gig really. It was a very strange setting.

PETER HOOK: There's very few sort of experiences you remember in your life that aren't sexual and I remember watching TV and I was just sat at home having my tea, Friday evening, I think it was, the Sex Pistols were on Granada. Oh my God. 'Anarchy In The UK', when Steve Jones threw a chair at Jordan. It was fantastic.

JORDAN: I think it was a great success. I think they [the Pistols] thought it was, but they were very disappointed about the audience and the atmosphere. But if you look at it, that's what makes it such a great performance.

The broadcast version of 'Anarchy In The UK' ends in a phase-out cacophony. Glen Matlock kicks over a mic stand and Jordan does The Twist on the stage. The last shot is of Rotten, staring at the cameramen for what seems to be an age, underscored by a few seconds of feedback and what sounds suspiciously like canned applause. It looks as if the tape has been tampered with. That's because it *had* been tampered with.

PETER WALKER: The original? That was edited slightly at the end. The real end of the number was totally different to what you see now. They started to kick the microphone stand around, kick the drums apart, kick the amplifiers over. They were doing a big job on their own kit on the stage. The young lady who was at the side with the armband on joined in. And I was under strict instructions not to show her at all on the television. The whole thing ended with all the chaos and all the gear falling apart with Rotten just staring into the lens. Really, really long, long stare. The audience was just totally silent. They didn't know whether to applaud or not. That look saved it, because what I could do then was go back and edit that look into the previous section, so it looked like the song was coming to an end. When, in actual fact, it never did.

JORDAN: The song overran – John wasn't ready to stop. He was giving quite a lot of verbal to the audience and knocking the stuff around. But he wasn't smashing the studio up. The equipment was getting knocked around a bit and he was getting really annoyed.

TONY WILSON: The studio audience of two hundred – even dumber hippies than me – sitting there for a music show, are also utterly flabbergasted. They'd rehearsed three-and-a-quarter minutes of this new song but, of course, they just went on and they went on and on and on. They did seven minutes and during the last two minutes they were kicking the set apart. As they hit the last chord, I'm sitting there with, obviously, a large grin on my face. The wonderful thing is, when the last note hits ... and stops ... there is complete silence. Two hundred people ... nothing ... just silence. Suddenly, you hear Chris Pye. He's running down from the control box and he's coming down the stairs to hit one of them for going three minutes over and kicking his set apart. They actually jump off stage and they run out the door. So by the time the producer arrives and says, 'Where the hell are they?!' they've gone – they've escaped. It was great.

PETER WALKER: That would be very typical of Chris Pye, to run down the stairs. He's a company man; he always was a company man. He knew that would reflect on his standing within Granada.

CHRIS PYE: I think I may have gone for a bit of a lie down at that stage. I felt really relieved it had finished and it was all over. I thought we had put something on the air that was so different and so extraordinary and that most people would find difficult and offensive and rude. I knew there'd be people complaining. You just knew the phones would be ringing when the show went out.

After the performance, Wilson states, 'Bakunin would have loved it, that was Sex Pistols, the leaders in their field.' For the uninitiated, Russian-born Mikhail Alexandrovich

Bakunin (1814–76) was one of the first generation of anarchist philosophers, considered one of the 'fathers of anarchy'. Nice one.

TONY WILSON: Why would Bakunin have loved it? Who said that? Did I say that? I can't believe I said that — did I say that? Oh God ... well, the idea that I am a posing bloody idiot is very correct. It's 'cause I loved it. I was always very proud they were on. It's good art. Bakunin *would* have loved it. Without a doubt. Great art. Groundbreaking, revolutionary, breaking down barriers. And shocking and upsetting and a great tune. A great tune and great art.

The end title music of *So It Goes* is 'Drift Away', as in 'I wanna get lost in your rock 'n' roll ... and drift away.' A caption appears proposing that 'One day, we'll look back on this and it will all seem funny...' The quote is attributed to Bruce Springsteen, 1973.

TONY WILSON: One of the things I liked most, looking back at that tape, is the line I say ... 'one of the most reviled phenomenon of recent weeks' ... and we're the other one, because everyone hated us ... and that's just the phrase of recent weeks. That's how absolutely current this moment was.

CHRIS PYE: I wasn't scared about the reaction, I just knew there'd *be* a reaction ... I wasn't scared about it, because we set the show up to do things that other people wouldn't do. Therefore, the fact that people were going to call in and complain was actually quite good news. At the end of the show, there was a sense of real elation. It wasn't just the elation that we'd managed to finish the show, it was elation that we put something on the air that was really, really extraordinary. Really, a wild moment of excitement.

PETER WALKER: At the time I didn't realise it was going to be a historical document. One of the reasons it became a historical document is, I think, a young chap called Julian Temple grabbed hold of it and used it in various films ... his *Great Rock 'n' Roll Swindle* and other feature films he made after that. If that hadn't happened, I don't think it would have become that much of a piece of footage.

CHRIS PYE: The bosses said to me, 'Who are they? ... What was that all about? They were bloody awful!' We had that kind of reaction. But nobody said to me, 'You should never have done that,' or, 'You made a mistake.' Everyone just said, 'Bloody hell, what was that?!'

PETER WALKER: After the performance, we invited everybody over to the green room to have a drink. We thought we'd better lock up the spirits and the heavy liquor, 'cause these guys are going to be trouble. After the programme, the Sex Pistols were in the corridor outside the room on the floor, sitting, just having a drink. We're all saying, 'Come on and join us.' They said, 'Oh no, we're all right here. Honest, we don't want to be any trouble.' They just sat there quietly drinking, never bothered a soul and afterwards said, 'Goodnight, thanks very much for the programme, hope to see you again Mr Walker.' Very nice.

GLEN MATLOCK: We did the show, that was that. Then we went off and had a drink in the dressing room. I came back to the studio 'cause I'd left me bass out there. There was this old boy sweeping up, must have been about sixty five. And he says, 'Were you in that band?' I says, 'Yeah, why?' I thought he was going to tick me off for being a young reprobate. He says, 'It's about fucking time that somebody fucking wound up those fucking bunch of fucking tossers. Good for you.'

JORDAN: I think that show in particular really stands the test of time, the part with the Sex Pistols in it. I think drawing the comparison between the bands that were on the show and the Pistols is just an amazing thing. It really does highlight just how far ahead of their time the Sex Pistols were and how it still lingers today in some forms.

That show was really groundbreaking ... there was, to my knowledge, nothing going on in London with Thames TV or any of the stations there at that time that could match it. So some transition had happened, be it to do with the Sex Pistols or that show ... or just the attitude of the people who live up there.

TONY WILSON: I'm proud of the seventy eight bands me and my colleagues put on television. But I'm really proud of bands we didn't ... 'cause we were right about them as well.

ALAN HEMSPALL: Three or four months later, Bill Grundy's TV show occurred. A few choice effing and jeffing moments on his show and suddenly they were news.

PHIL SINGLETON: Grundy certainly created more of an impact in the national press. I think it changed punk. For the better? Possibly not, but it changed its evolution into something which, ultimately, wasn't as healthy. The Grundy interview led to the demise of the Sex Pistols very quickly. Within fourteen months that was it, as a direct result of the Grundy show.

JORDAN: John [Rotten] was quite an introverted person, not the sort of guy who'd like to go out clubbing, he was quite a quiet, thinking person, quite unlike Steve who was a bit of a lad. I think that comes through very obviously, when they're on stage, they've all got their own little character to play.

PETER WALKER: I met Johnny Rotten years later and he was just the same. He was still a nice bloke. That's the thing, when you look at the footage ... he is a nice bloke and then something takes hold of him. A demon takes hold of him.

CHRIS PYE: I was the wrong generation. Maybe if I'd been fifteen years younger. I didn't really realise at that stage how

punk rock was going to become the enormous style movement that it did. It wasn't clear then, so I didn't know that this
was a moment which was going to define music television.

He's right. Hindsight can be a wonderful thing. It's not
always easy to spot the cultural importance of something
as it's sneaking up on you. Or even if it's making a mess of
your television studio. I'll give you an example: it's from the
New Musical Express Book Of Rock 2, published in 1977 –
a hefty paperback A–Z guide to rock 'n' roll. It would have
been collated at just around this time: September 1976.
Under P for Punk there is a page about the 1960s stylings of
The Standells, ? & the Mysterians, The 13th Floor Elevators
and the *Nuggets* compilation. It then states, 'Punk rock
revived as a popular term in the Seventies, though in a much
more loosely defined context, to refer to US acts like Bruce
Springsteen, Patti Smith and, particularly, Nils Lofgren; in
the UK London bands like Eddie And The Hot Rods helped
initiate new punk-rock vogue.'

That's not the view from the showbiz pages of the *Daily
Mail*, that's the *NME Book of Rock*, written in the latter
part of 1976. Even *they* missed it by a nautical mile, so
be wary of those who claim they spotted the Zeitgeist just
as the wave was preparing to crest, grabbed their cultural
surfboards and rode that baby right onto the Beach of
Rock. *Never* trust them.

Hindsight, you see. Wonderful thing.

Issue 8 of *Penetration Magazine*, featuring Kiss and Sex Pistols
... a more unlikely pairing you never did see.   © *Paul Welsh*

CHAPTER SEVEN

I'M ALREADY
A HAS-BEEN

By 8 October 1976 the Sex Pistols had signed a £40,000 contract with EMI. The relationship wasn't going to last long – they would end up at Virgin via A&M – but, from that point onward, the Sex Pistols were part of the music industry. That industry and, more importantly, the way we access it was about to totally change, thanks to the next move planned by Buzzcocks. Six months after their first real gig at the Lesser Free Trade Hall, the entrepreneurial Buzzcocks became the first punk band to set up their own record label. In January 1977 they released the *Spiral Scratch* EP on the New Hormones label. It was £1 a pop. The distance between the band and the audience – which had been taken in, like Howard Devoto's trousers, as a result of the Lesser Free Trade Hall – had just become even narrower.

HOWARD DEVOTO: The idea of doing our own record label, New Hormones, I wouldn't say that came from the Pistols in any sense. They'd signed to EMI by the time we were getting *Spiral Scratch* together. By then, Stiff Records had started. I did have a word with Dave Robinson [head of Stiff Records] when we were trying to pull that together, to see whether he had any helpful advice. I don't recall him having any helpful advice whatsoever – he was kind of vaguely encouraging. I think that the second gig was perhaps particularly impactful. Because of what people saw that night, they didn't only see the Sex Pistols, they saw Buzzcocks, who were a local group. I think that actually had a big impact on people.

JORDAN: Buzzcocks are still one of my favourite bands. I did a lot of gigs with them and with Adam And The Ants and I thought they were great – probably the best to come out in the wake of the Pistols – but Buzzcocks were in a different league really. They had the same independence and the same power but they'd made something new out of it and it wasn't just a re-hash. I really didn't like The Clash very much – I think that they preached a sort of poverty-stricken, downtrodden story in their songs, nothing heroic. Just something you don't want to hear in a song, I'm afraid. I didn't like them for that. It's almost like taking being working-class to its real extremes. Well, the Pistols didn't need to say that they were working-class. If you need to state it, you've got a chip on your shoulder in some way, which is what I think separated bands like The

Clash. X-Ray Spex were a great band too. They were really wonderful, I loved them and Buzzcocks, but for a different reason. Buzzcocks had some great lyrics as well and they were great guys and, do you know, I often sing their songs in the bathroom ... still [laughing].

HOWARD DEVOTO: It was a big deal to borrow money from your friends and to go through the whole thing and go to a vaguely proper recording studio and have records made and then give them to shops and start talking 'wholesale price'. I remember Malcolm [McLaren] saying to me when he first saw *Spiral Scratch* in Rough Trade or Bizarre Records, the handful of shops that were stocking it, he was saying, it's quite odd seeing this record, that has come from nowhere.

PETE SHELLEY: Our agent wanted to become a record producer, so he called himself Martin Zero instead of Martin Hannett. We believed him when he said that he was a record producer – we were just as gullible as everybody else. Instead of going to the record company, cap in hand, or trying to get an A&R guy to go come up to Manchester, you decided you don't need that and you just did it yourself. He [Hannett] suggested making a record. He thought he could get some studio time, some down-time at a studio. So because of that, it wasn't going to cost us anything. But all that fell through, so then we started researching, well, how would you go and make a record? We found we could get a thousand copies done for five hundred quid.

HOWARD DEVOTO: We had to learn it ourselves, piece it together: where could you get records pressed? How do you go about doing it? Have we really got to settle for those injection-moulded ones, where you didn't get a proper stick-on label either? They were the only ones that would press a small run of a thousand singles or maybe they were a little bit cheaper or something because there wasn't a stick-on label. Maybe it was Martin Hannett – I think he may have had some contact, because he was really pretty new to it as well.

PETE SHELLEY: I might have still been sat in Leigh, playing in my bedroom thinking, 'Ooh, if only I can get a record company to listen to my music.' It's almost like the Gordian Knot, which Alexander had so intricately tied and nobody could undo it. He just got his knife and sliced it in two and solved the problem. By exercising your will, you can make things happen. So everything which has happened since is as a direct result of that.

The EP was funded by money begged and borrowed from friends and family by Devoto and Richard Boon, a former school friend who had now become Buzzcocks' manager. From office space housed with the now-defunct listings magazine *New Manchester Review*, they worked out they needed to sell 600 copies to break even. Ambitiously, the EP had a picture cover, with the band snapped on Polaroid in Manchester's Piccadilly Gardens. They only had two chances to take the cover shot as the camera only had two frames left. On the first, Devoto had his eyes closed. The second and final shot was used on the cover. Each vinyl disc was put in each sleeve by hand.

STEVE DIGGLE: I remember bringing my dad's car to this industrial estate in Salford to pick up these thousand records. All the rest of the stuff in the warehouse was washing machines and stuff. It was weird to see what a thousand records looked like. Not that much, actually. It was a massive thing for us and usurped the whole thing about the record industry – and they got worried. We didn't need them anymore. The first home-made, do-it-yourself punk record in the country.

HOWARD DEVOTO: I think *Spiral Scratch* really turned around Buzzcocks' career. One of the reasons we did our own record was the fact we were in Manchester. There were no record companies. It wasn't like we could even find that many gigs to play. There weren't record-company people coming up, the music papers weren't coming up, we had to do it ourselves. We pressed a thousand, we had no idea whether we'd even sell a thousand. We ended up selling sixteen thousand.

The EP's running order is 'Breakdown', 'Times Up', 'Boredom' and 'Friends Of Mine'. 'Boredom' is the standout track, with its two-note guitar solo and rumbling bass. Devoto's nasal, sneery vocal sounds like a spoof of Cockney Rebel lead singer Steve Harley, rather than a homage to Johnny Rotten. At one stage he declares, 'I'm already a has-been'.

A matter of days after *Spiral Scratch* hit the shops, Howard Devoto upped and left Buzzcocks. It seemed a perverse act for a man who had achieved so much in the space of just six months. Devoto's departure from Buzzcocks sent a genuine shock through Manchester's post-Free Trade Hall music scene. There was disbelief in the music press too but seemingly no bitterness from his band-mates. Pete Shelley, who had sung with his schoolboy band Jets Of Air, took over on vocals. Four weeks later they made their live debut as Buzzcocks – minus Howard Devoto.

PETE SHELLEY: He was in his final year at college and there was no future in what we were doing. It was just a bit of fun. Bit like your mum calling you in 'cause your tea's ready.

STEVE DIGGLE: We used to rehearse at Howard's house – he had this monitor lizard, fucking thing hissing at you while you were playing. I hated that fucking lizard – we finished rehearsing and me and Pete were sat on the couch and he said, 'I've done what I wanted to do and made a record and now I'm leaving the band.' It was kind of a shock and a surprise you know ... for about two minutes ... and then we thought, 'Well, we'll carry on.'

HOWARD DEVOTO: I felt at the time that, having recorded the record, that's maybe as far as it could go for me. I'd now seen through quite a lot of the whole process of being in a band, playing a gig and then making a record. I was in the middle of my Humanities degree and, having buggered up my Psychology one and the thick end of my school career as well, I wasn't that wild to go on perpetuating my failures in the academic department.

STEVE DIGGLE: It became a bit more accessible when Howard left – and we became a good-looking group. John Maher on drums, Steve Garvey on bass, me on guitar and Pete ... it was a good-looking group. You've got to have a bit of sex in a group. We were singing about an Orgasm Addict, which turned the birds on. A lot of girls started coming. We looked kind of sexy, whereas Howard ... [laughs] ... he was more a *mysterious* version of sexy.

HOWARD DEVOTO: I was not fantastically taken, I suppose, with the *aesthetic* of it all. I wasn't that wild about the vibe and ambience of it in a way – it didn't feel exactly musically right for me at the end of January 1977. Not that I can say I was sure at that time that I'd even go on to be in another band.

But he did go on to be in another band – Magazine. And with the formation of that group came one of rock music's great pieces of sleight of hand: Howard Devoto became post-punk before most people had even cut their hair and become punks.

ALAN HEMPSALL: I was stood at the Elizabethan Hall at Belle Vue [Manchester], watching Magazine's first gig. It became apparent that this man had been in a punk band but had ditched it fast. Now there was a new phase and I think that's the thing that people forget about punk. It wasn't the item in itself, it was the fact that it was a precursor to, and a catalyst for, what was to come. And that was the real meat and two veg. Punk had done its job. It had got rid of all the crap and the pretentiousness.

STEVE SHY: Everyone had to get involved. I did a fanzine called *Shy Talk*. It came about because I was talking to Richard Boon and Pete Shelley at a gig. They said, 'You've got to start a band.' Now, I'm tone deaf, but Pete said that doesn't matter. So instead we decided to do a fanzine. The first one was 1976 – probably about three months after the Pistols gig. To be honest it was absolutely crap, but it gave Paul Morley a chance to get on the ladder – he used to write for it. It gave somewhere for [Manchester music photographer] Kevin Cummins to get his photos in. It supposedly got Steven Morris his job drumming in Joy Division after we put a piece in saying they wanted a drummer.

Audience member Paul Morley would soon graduate from being a fanzine scribbler on the likes of *Penetration* and *Shy Talk* to *New Musical Express* contributor, firing off dispatches on the Manchester scene to London.

PAUL MORLEY: Howard Devoto seemed like an incredibly mesmeric presence. Afterwards, when he did Magazine and we wrote about him being the most important man alive, a lot of Londoners were a bit confused as to why we'd said this. We said it in a way, not necessarily just for the music, but because we knew that this man was responsible for bringing the Pistols up to Manchester. And that was just the beginning of everything that Manchester has since become ... even within three years it seemed important, let alone all these years later.

Suddenly, across Manchester, there were places that bands could play that didn't require you to be hugely famous or American. Venues like The Ranch, Pips, Rafters and The Electric Circus in Collyhurst all played their part in creating what the city had lacked for so many years: a scene.

PAUL MORLEY: You were going to see bands like The Fall, from Manchester, *in Manchester*. You were seeing Joy Division in Manchester, you were seeing Buzzcocks, you know, from Manchester, in Manchester. Suddenly you had a little scene; clearly created by other people that were at the two Sex Pistols' concerts.

PETER HOOK: We had a meeting with Pete Shelley in a pub in Broughton [an area of Salford, Greater Manchester] to ask him how we should form a band. God, amazing! *And he told us.*

HOWARD DEVOTO: The Fall were pretty quick on the scene. I remember going along to the art centre and seeing them within, must have been, maybe a couple of months after that second gig.

Docks clerk Mark Edward Smith, from Sedgely Park in Salford, formed The Fall as a bedroom poetry band after seeing the Sex Pistols at the Lesser Free Trade Hall. Their style was a clattering marriage of psychobilly beats and chants, overlaid by Smith's often impenetrable preacher-man tirades. He sang of witches, bingo masters and elastic men. Baffling, yet strangely compelling.

MARK E. SMITH: We thought punk sold out very quickly and it rapidly became sped-up heavy metal bands and blokes with skinny ties. That's what got us going more. The initial promise of the Pistols wasn't really fulfilled. It went down very quickly. So we thought we'd better do something about it. The whole idea of The Fall was already being nurtured, unconsciously. It was to write intelligent lyrics to very basic music. We wanted to be a bit more esoteric. The Fall were very, very young compared to the Pistols. In a way, they became the establishment very quickly. That's what we felt at the time. When it kicked off, the thing with punk was that it was 'working-class' music. But, in fact, it wasn't. The Sex Pistols were on Virgin for Christ's sake – they were the enemy as far as me and my friends were concerned.

PAUL MORLEY: Well, it happened very quickly and very naturally. There were really important bands like The Fall and the strange Warsaw/Joy Division sort of area. Even bands that seemed to sort of be crappy. There was a great band called The Worst, who were a couple of mechanics from Rochdale. They did their gigs in the same clothes they used to fix the cars and the drummer had a kid's drum kit that he held together with bricks. The bass player never had his bass plugged in and, to me, they were the great lost punk group. I'd be surprised if they weren't there, at least at that second Sex Pistols show. They were fantastic and all their songs were about the police state and lasted about thirty seconds and then just disintegrated. But there were incredible bands like The Fall who happened very quickly.

STEVE SHY: I managed The Worst for a while. They'd put on gigs and it cost a toy to get in. The toys would go to the local kids' hospital.

PETER HOOK: We preferred bands like The Worst – they couldn't play. One had the drum kit and one had the guitar and they just used to rant and rave. Oh, it was great. And he'd smash his kit up at the end. The second gig we did, they played with us. Great days.

The Worst's Alan Deaves and Ian Hodges would gain further notoriety by appearing in a Manchester-produced BBC TV documentary/discussion show about punk for the *Brass Tacks* current affairs series. The show saw the likes of Pete Shelley, John Peel and Steve Shy putting the case for the positive aspects of punk, while local councillors from up and down the land denounced the movement, described as being 'a bigger threat to our way of life than Russian communism or hyper-inflation.' Footage from the show has cropped up repeatedly over the years in punk documentaries. Cameras followed local punk girl Denise Shaw to work and as she got ready for a night out and Pastor John Copper invited the punks to repent to the Lord Jesus Christ. Steve Shy was filmed in his bedroom, putting together the latest edition of *Shy Talk*.

STEVE SHY: I thought the programme was well done in the way that it showed that, underneath it all, we were nice people. We won the audience over at the time, which could have saved a few punks from getting battered.

DAWN BRADBURY: I thought the *Brass Tacks* show was great. They followed Denise Shaw to work. Her company got phone calls the next day from people saying they should sack her. She's an abomination. She's got pink hair. Where are we at today? Everybody's got pink hair! 'You must sack that girl from her job.' How appalling. How narrow-minded.

The fact that the BBC documentary was set in Manchester showed how the city had taken punk to its collective heart. Even audience member Jon the Postman got in on the act – literally. As well as producing his own fanzine, his other method of diminishing the distance between band and audience was to invade the stage at the end of an increasing number of punk gigs and commandeer the microphone, treating the audience to an a cappella assault.

JON THE POSTMAN: I didn't have it in my head to form a band after I'd seen them [the Sex Pistols]. In fact, I have no idea why I got on stage that night at a Buzzcocks gig at the Band On The Wall in 1977. Most probably because I was drunk and I thought, 'Well, there's an attitude here, there's microphones here, the band had left the stage and I will make my statement.'

The Postman's weapon of choice was 'Louie Louie' by The Kingsmen, one of the earliest examples of US garage punk.

JON THE POSTMAN: That was my favourite punk anthem, you know, of the 1960s. The simplest song you can sing.

ALAN HEMPSALL: I think the grimness was just something that was there in Manchester in the late 1970s. There were several ways you could deal with it and you could look at the way The Fall produced things or Joy Division, those kinds of bands. They all had a different way of portraying that. You could say that Mark E. Smith and The Fall had a more tongue-in-cheek approach, more of a witty approach than Joy Division.

By the start of 1977, what had begun as Peter Hook and Bernard Sumner's experiment in wrecking Grandma's radiogram had developed into a band. After toying with the name Stiff Kittens, thanks to an idea by Buzzcocks' manager Richard Boon, they settled on Warsaw, inspired by the David Bowie track 'Warsawa' on his *Low* album. Ian Curtis, from Hurdsfield in Macclesfield, a fair distance from Manchester and the nascent scene, was on vocals. Without a regular drummer, their debut was at The Electric Circus in Manchester in May 1977, supporting Buzzcocks.

PETER HOOK: We did a gig with Buzzcocks at The Electric Circus and Pete Shelley said to the audience [affects camp voice], 'Now, stop spitting all of you, please ... stop. We're not playing any more till you stop spitting,' so they all stopped. And he went, 'Right, now that's better ... one, two, three, four,' and they all spat at him! Oh God, fantastic moments in punk history. By God, it was amazing.

JOHN BERRY (early roadie): Warsaw were universally panned. They were shit! In terms of music at the time, they were fucking shit. They couldn't play a note and didn't know what they were doing.

As 1977 turned into 1978, and with an EP called *An Ideal For Living* recorded, Warsaw became Joy Division. The band's name – called after the sterilised Nazi labour-camp sex slaves featured in the 1955 novel *The House of Dolls* – and the Hitler Youth drummer-boy design of the sleeve, made it look like the band were purposely asking to be disliked.

BERNARD SUMNER: The climate was very different in those days. It was the time of punk and shock, sticking two fingers up to what we regarded as normal society – and that included some journalists. We knew the name was on dodgy ground and we did have some reservations about it – but in the end it just felt like it was our name. It's very difficult to explain but at the time we did everything at the time with instinct not intellect and, when you do that, it's very difficult to know when to let intellect intervene and abandon your instinct.

PAUL MORLEY: The punky, gobbie side of it was just sort of the way it got transformed by the tabloid world, people jumping on it thinking that it was simpler and sillier than it actually was. So it kind of split very quickly into two sides. There was that silly side that, for me, Slaughter And The Dogs predicted and there was the side that actually influenced all music and pop culture.

DAWN BRADBURY: People who allegedly jumped on the bandwagon were already in bands. They found punk music, understood its appeal and decided they wanted to play it. Gary Callender, who went with us to the first gig, was playing in a middle-of-the-road rock band. Long hair, scruffy jeans, Jesus sandals, the usual attire and the usual music. All of a sudden ... he found affinity.

He became Gus Gangrene in Manchester punk band The Drones.

PETER HOOK: It did fragment a little bit. Tony Wilson tried his best to pull it together. God, he was the first middle-class person I ever talked to. Buzzcocks were quite middle-class, so I don't think they could relate to our beer-boy attitude, when they were quite a bit art school. It was very difficult for me to sit in the same room with Howard Devoto, because we absolutely had nothing in common in life apart from the fact that we were in a group. It was difficult for us as a group, because we weren't arty enough. We sort of fell out of the punk thing – it got a bit too arty; it wasn't punky enough for us.

The 'beer-boys' of Joy Division were perceived very differently by the music press. Largely through their uncommunicative interviews and the icy photographs taken of the band to accompany them, they came to be seen as aloof, with a doomed grandeur. The truth couldn't be further away.

PETER HOOK: I remember the first gig we did as Joy Division, which was at Pips [a former underground disco on Fennel Street near Manchester Cathedral]. That was the biggest fight I'd ever seen in my life. It was great. Every gig was just like a massive release of energy.

PAUL MORLEY: The image now tends to be the punks on the King's Road with the spiky hair and the chains and the leather jackets but it was actually a really intellectual, literate movement. You think of the Buzzcocks' songs that Howard Devoto wrote, they were incredibly literate; and Johnny Rotten's lyrics were incredibly literate; The Fall were incredibly literate; Joy Division – incredibly sophisticated and complex.

Other bands were appearing on the circuit too: the shouty yet disciplined Drones and Ed Banger And The Nosebleeds, who were just plain shouty.

EDDIE GARRITY: There was definitely a big change then, because we were just plodding, just doing the odd gigs up in Stalybridge and Ashton [in east Manchester] to about fifteen people. And immediately we became a punk band and had a single out, it was like four hundred people at a concert, which was like ridiculous really, 'cause no one had heard us up to that day. So being a punk band just upped the ante so much; there was so much interest in it.

JON THE POSTMAN: The Nosebleeds played The Electric Circus and Paul Morley didn't like them at all – he was heckling in a rather vociferous way and Eddie Garrity got off stage and pummelled his head in. I was stood quite near him at the time. I actually thought they were quite amusing, because they were the biggest laugh ... in the way they transcended it because they were entertaining.

After the Pistols' appearance on the last episode of the series, the *So It Goes* team grabbed hold of punk and the 'new wave' that was already tailgating it and bunged as many bands onto the television as possible. Out went the comedy, poetry and faffing about, in came music, music, music.

CHRIS PYE: Because we'd put the first bit of punk on television, I think there was a natural instinct that we were on a cutting edge so that we should do more of it. Punk was getting bigger.

TONY WILSON: I waited for a year, shivering with nightmares, that someone at the BBC or elsewhere would wake up and put all these bands on. Luckily, the man at the BBC thought it was all about technique so, unless you were technically proficient or American, you couldn't go on *The Old Grey Whistle Test*. What a dickhead. Wonderful for us. Through the autumn and the spring of 1977, we were able to put bands on at Granada: Slaughter, Buzzcocks, The Jam and The Clash and everything. We were just very lucky that the rest of the world was dumb.

JON THE POSTMAN: The first time I saw Tony Wilson at a punk gig was May or June 1977 when he actually filmed me. He came down with a camera crew from *So It Goes* and he wanted to film me singing a cappella, because he'd heard about this mad guy who got on stage by himself. And he got absolutely drenched with urine, spit and plenty of stale beer that night. In fact, people were chanting the theme from *The Old Grey Whistle Test*.

PETER WALKER: It took the development of the Sex Pistols idea and amplified it, in some cases, *ad nauseum*. It became the same programme really, every week, and it was an explosion of punk which drove it. The worst highlight I remember seeing was Tony's idea – a thinking man's intuition about music – this 'let's go down the clubs and see blokes gobbing at groups' type of programme. And, of course, that's what Julian Temple did, very cleverly, with the footage [from *So It Goes*]. He intercut it with footage of blokes gobbing on the stage and it looked like they were performing in front of an audience. But, of course, that didn't happen – the gobbing wasn't there.

The footage shot for the second series of *So It Goes* would form the backbone of every punk-related music documentary for decades. If you see early footage of Buzzcocks, The Banshees, Penetration or The Jam, you can pretty much guarantee that it came from *So It Goes* series two. In much of the 'let's go down the clubs' footage from the second series of *So It Goes*, a distinctive youth can be clearly seen at the very front of the stage. Red of face and of hair – a young Mick Hucknall is unmistakable, shaking a sweaty, ginger head. By the turn of the decade he'd formed the punkish Frantic Elevators, before becoming Simply Red. The *So It Goes* recordings were compiled into a series for Sky Arts in 2014 called *Anarchy In Manchester*. Despite being a groundbreaking pre-cursor to everything from *The Tube* to *Later... with Jools Holland*, the series was frowned upon by Granada bosses and film of a sweary Iggy Pop performing at the Manchester Apollo in 1977 proved to be the last straw and the show was axed.

TONY WILSON: In the middle of 'The Passenger' he yelled out 'fucking'. There was a week's debate about this one word. I'm screaming, 'ART! ART! IT'S FUCKING ART!' They'd had enough of me and I can't blame them.

Although still holding down his straight job as a TV news presenter by day, Tony Wilson now had time on his hands thanks to Iggy Pop. So he started Factory Records, named after a post-punk music night at the Russell Club on Royce Road in Hulme, a former social club for bus drivers. With their New Hormones label, Buzzcocks had shown that independence could be achieved. Early Factory releases came from a broad church: the ambient noodling of Durutti Column; the anorexic funk of A Certain Ratio; the beer-boy doom of Joy Division; and the Wirral electronica of former prog-rockers Orchestral Manoeuvres In The Dark.

TONY WILSON: Punk created ... allowed ... a whole other era of music – Elvis Costello, post-punk – in which some of the high art is dropped. Joy Division, Elvis Costello or U2 doesn't happen without the flame, without the Pistols, without the explosion, without punk.

PETE SHELLEY: I think that gig at the Lesser Free Trade Hall was more or less the seed. It started a lot of things off. But, of course, me and Howard knew no one at all in Manchester. The only people we knew who were interested in the kind of music we were into were the Sex Pistols. I had no knowledge of the scene, if there was one. There'd been no sense of direction or purpose in it, and then suddenly there was. And it was basically 'you can do it', so everybody started doing 'it' and surprisingly 'it' worked out.

Before starting Factory, Tony Wilson had taken a great deal of interest in Rabid Records – Martin Hannett, producer of *Spiral Scratch*, was heavily involved with the label. Slaughter And The Dogs were one of their first signings and released their rock-a-boogie anthem 'Cranked Up Really High' as their first single. All power chords and drawling vocals, Slaughter can still remember the day they took delivery of the first batch.

MICK ROSSI: Just the coolest feeling in the world. I had to take it out of the sleeve, in and out about eight times, put it down, pick it up, look at it. You'd look at this piece of plastic and it would have 'Cranked Up Really High' by Barrett and Rossi. Then I'd pick up 'Jean Jeanie' [David Bowie] ... like the kid in you.

WAYNE BARRETT: For me, it was like that Neil Armstrong thing, I swear to God, you know, it's like putting a flag on the moon.

Either the laddish Joy Division boys were superb actors or the music press of the period conspired to hide their true characters. Either way, the ethereal image that was foisted upon them worked wonders. Britain was enthralled by the band and their debut album for Factory Records, *Unknown Pleasures*, in 1979. But when lead singer Ian Curtis committed suicide in the early hours of 18 May 1980, the early image of the band created by the press was preserved in amber for good. But it also starkly highlighted the fact that, if the intensity of the music and the level of expectation were going to be this costly, it probably wasn't worth it.

Although the wave of emotion over Curtis's death inadvertently made a great success of the material released directly afterwards, particularly the single 'Love Will Tear Us Apart', the whole scene needed to back off and rethink.

Buzzcocks' post-Devoto success as a pop act effectively removed them from that scene, as Pete Shelley steered them towards the charts with singles like 'What Do I Get?', 'I Don't Mind' and 'Ever Fallen in Love (With Someone You Shouldn't've)?' Barely a week seemed to go by without seeing Pete winsomely leading the band through another faultless slab of punk pop on *Top Of The Pops*, his head always feyly tilted to one side as he told of his latest lovelorn woes. Their old muckers Slaughter And The Dogs had, by now, signed to Decca and, in a spoof of the Sex Pistols signing their contract with A&M outside Buckingham Palace, put their signatures to the deal outside Wythenshawe dole office. But away from the independent spirit of Rabid, Barrett struggled with the business-like environment of a 'proper' record company. So he did what any Wythenshawe lad does in a tricky situation ... he did a bunk.

WAYNE BARRETT: I think it was the business side basically. For me, as an artist, I liked to dream. I like to think freely and do basically what I want. If I can't do that, it's not worth continuing. I was happy with Mike [Mick Rossi], we were the best of friends, Mr Rossi and myself. We've known each other since we were kids. Other people from the outside were coming in and destroying things. I think it became a little bit too commercial. I mean, we were in it for the money as well, but we were in it for having a good time firstly. If we make money out of it, that's the reward of fame. We wanted to do just 'local famous'. When it became kind of national, people came in from the outside and started distorting it. And that's why I buggered off to France.

MICK ROSSI: At the time I was incredibly hurt. But at the same time, I knew it was on the cards in a weird way, like a sixth-sense type thing. Looking back on it, it's like it was a necessary evil for that to happen because, coming full circle, it's stronger and the bond is tighter than ever, which makes me happy. But at the time, I was hurt.

With commitments to fulfil, Rossi found a replacement in the young man off whose head a bottle went 'ping' at the second Sex Pistols gig at the Lesser Free Trade Hall. Eddie Garrity, aka Ed Banger.

EDDIE GARRITY: I joined Slaughter in late 1979 after Wayne had run off. I got a phone call and joined them within two days, because I already knew the songs from way back. Just a matter of stepping in at two days' notice and straight into the tour. We did the album and a couple of singles, but we split up again.

MICK ROSSI: It was really like, OK, who can we get? We've got to do this record, do we carry on? Yeah, I think we can carry on. What about Eddie from Ed Banger And The Nosebleeds? Eddie's a really nice man and I think it was terrific of him to step into such big shoes ... it wasn't the same.

With the new Slaughter not really gelling, Rossi cast around for other collaborators. Billy Duffy, later of The Cult, was drafted in. So was a young man who'd attended the first Lesser Free Trade Hall gig and taken the trouble to 'pen an epistle' about it to the music press.

MICK ROSSI: Wayne had actually gone underground – I didn't know where he was. I'd gone to another record company and started working with Billy and Billy says, 'I know this great singer called Morrissey.' So I said, 'OK, we'll give that a shot.' So we had a few rehearsals and I felt Morrissey was incredibly talented as a lyric writer, but then he was very introverted. He was this shy man, you had to prize him out of his shell, he didn't have a lot to say. Being exposed to Morrissey at this early stage, before he blossomed into what he is today, was interesting too. In a weird way it was never anything to do with Slaughter ... it was just kind of on the sideline.

Morrissey And The Dogs. Things could have been so different. Steven Patrick Morrissey – or 'the Stretford Schoolboy', as Tony Wilson always insisted on calling him – would have been one of the younger members of the audience when the Sex Pistols played in Manchester in June 1976. Morrissey saw the Pistols three times in Manchester in 1976 – he'd later describe them as 'Not the saviours of culture, but the destruction of it ... their immediate success is an exhilarating danger to behold.' He went on to front The Smiths, probably the most important group of the 1980s. He'd already been a temporary member of an Ed Banger-less Nosebleeds before his link up with Slaughter. It seems mighty strange now to think that the fey wordsmith, who would invite you to 'pin and mount me like a butterfly' in The Smiths' song 'Reel Around The Fountain', once held his own with south-Manchester toughs like Slaughter and the Nosebleeds. It's an indication, if nothing else, of his eagerness to succeed.

Even stage-invading Jon the Postman branched out, graduating from guerrilla-style performances of 'Louie Louie' to actually being asked to perform with bands like The Fall and The Drones. God help us, he eventually released three albums of his own.

JON THE POSTMAN: Well, Dave Bentley, the manager of The Drones, he took a chance and said, 'Do you fancy coming on the scene? I will pay for the studio and I'll pay for the pressing and the distribution.' So he arranged it all and I recorded my first album [*Puerile*] in February 1978. Which was a fine day.

Joy Division's answer to the weighty expectation that surrounded them was to become New Order ... and to dance. After initially testing the waters as a three-piece, drummer Stephen Morris's girlfriend Gillian Gilbert was recruited and they had their first hit with 'Ceremony' in 1981. The following year saw an inspirational visit to New York and the band brought home the idea of a NYC-style disco to the grey streets of Manchester. Inspired by clubs like Danceteria, The Funhouse and The Paradise Garage – and struggling to find something to do with the unexpected cash generated by their single 'Love Will Tear Us Apart' – New Order and Factory Records found an ex-boat showroom on Whitworth Street West and turned it into The Haçienda. Its grey-and-yellow interior was designed by Ben Kelly, who also helped create interiors at a shop at 430 King's Road in London, former business address of one Malcolm McLaren ... positively serpentine, these Lesser Free Trade Hall connections.

Using the subtitle of 'FAC 51', as it was the fifty-first thing produced by Factory, it opened on 21 May 1982. Stars of the day, like Martin Fry of ABC and Ian McCulloch of Echo And The Bunnymen, were there on that fateful evening. But after an initial flurry of interest, the club soon slumped.

Nobody used to go to The Haçienda in its early, pre-dance phase. The sound was awful, the silvery-grey paint came off on your clothes and you could only get in with a credit card-style membership thing, which all the wreckheads promptly lost immediately after being issued them. My friends and I used to go to The Haçienda some Saturday nights if we were tired and wanted somewhere to have a sit down. As a gig venue, it just about got away with it, with some key performances by The Smiths and New Order. The rest of the time it was the likes of proto-goths, Bauhaus, The Birthday Party and McLaren protégés Bow Wow Wow that filled the diary. It's a period in the club's history that tends to be conveniently washed over in retrospectives about the Greatest Club In The World. It was more like an indulgent arts centre than a centre of decadence – they even sold sandwiches at lunchtime.

But The Haçienda was saved thanks to the other thing that New Order brought back from New York along with the idea of a big, flouncy discotheque in the middle of Manchester: electro beats. Big shiny ones that you could see your face in ... and dance your arse off to. New Order jettisoned everything bar Peter Hook's low-slung bass lines in favour of sequencers, drum machines and spidery, one-fingered synthesiser melodies. Adopting and adapting Kraftwerk via Africa Bambaataa – Trans Pennine Express, if you will – New Order made it OK for white boys to dance again. A vital leap that paved the way for the Madchester scene and a contribution which seals their influence and importance far more firmly and securely than Joy Division's. Bernard Sumner would do an extraordinary thing with New Order – replace a singer who has died and make the resulting band even more successful. And with the release of the album *Power, Corruption And Lies*, and of the 12-inch electro workout 'Blue Monday' in 1983, New Order also helped keep the doors of the ailing Haçienda open.

BERNARD SUMNER: It was like the Beatles' Apple label. But we weren't The Beatles and didn't have their money! I think this is why we were pushed out on tours of the States so much. It was the only way for us to receive some money – our royalties were being wasted on The Haçienda.

'Blue Monday' spent over thirty weeks in the charts and became the best-selling 12-inch single of all-time, though Factory Records' legend would have it that the band lost money on it thanks to the Fancy Dan packaging. The more they sold, the more money they lost. Apparently.

TERRY MASON: It's a good story. Factory had a lot of stories that leave you chortling and deflect you away from other stuff that was going on. The first batch will have lost money, but there's always someone who will do it 10p cheaper. Factory, Joy Division, New Order ... it's just a myth business, isn't it? Tony Wilson had lots of stories he could roll out and people like stories. The truth? People can take or leave that. Don't spoil a good story by putting in the truth.

BERNARD SUMNER: Only Tony knows the truth behind this legend...

Whether it was money or sheer bloody-mindedness that kept the doors open, the club managed to bridge the lean years before acid house and rave culture made The Haçienda and Madchester the place to be.

It also proved that the often sexually and culturally incompatible bedfellows of rock and dance could do it together. Dance nights at The Haçienda took over as the most popular events, pushing the mooching goths and the indie-rock boys elsewhere. A barely used counselling drug, 3,4-methylenedioxymethamphetamine, or MDMA, became the stimulant of choice. The baby-acid drug known as ecstasy made everything sound great, Factory signings Happy Mondays – essentially Slaughter And The Dogs on ecstasy – came up with the album *Bummed*, produced by Martin Hannett. Unlike Joy Division, the Mondays didn't need journalists to mould a suitable image for them. Their loping dance-skiffle and dealer-chic casual look was enough to make them Factory's next act to make the music press surrender without struggle. When the band appeared on the same edition of *Top Of The Pops* as The Stone Roses and Manc duo Candy Flip, that was pretty much all you needed to know about Madchester in one easy, half-hour lesson. The Roses, former goth moochers from the posher suburbs of south Manchester had tagged a 'Funky Drummer' beat onto their slightly winsome Jangledelica and had hoovered up the teenage vote, enamoured with their stand-alone swagger. Candy Flip's dreamy cover of 'Strawberry Fields Forever' was made all the dreamier with the knowledge that their name was a slang expression for an LSD/MDMA double dose. Even former Factory signings James traded in the majority of their beardy-folk for a slice of the dance action with 'Sit Down' – essentially a T-shirt with the option to buy a single of the same name.

Rock and dance had come together and formed a coalition. Without that truce, the connection to the Lesser Free Trade Hall would have been severed and the seeds sown by the Pistols would have died. The Haçienda would have withered on the vine before being resuscitated by the dance boom. The appropriation of shiny beats by two Salford lads who started out on Grandma's stereo after seeing the Sex Pistols in 1976 had saved the day. Manchester's stranglehold on popular music and its attached culture was able to continue in the 1990s, where, ironically, the beats were replaced by the dull, returning thud of distorted guitars.

TONY WILSON: Youth cultural revolutions – for me, they're the greatest things. There was an old sound guy at Granada in Manchester, who was a lovely old geezer. He once said to me, 'I went to record The Beatles at the Cavern, in late 1962. I've got the tape of it.' He brought the tape in. And you know what it sounded just like? The Pistols at the Free Trade Hall in 1976. It's got that energy and reality. Whenever there's a youth revolution, the people in charge of the media who've grown up in the last one say, 'This is quite interesting, but not as good as the last one.' That's bollocks: they're all equally valuable. Acid House was as good as punk and punk was as good as Merseybeat. They're all fantastic moments of renewal.

JON THE POSTMAN: If it wouldn't have been the Pistols, it would have been us, or somebody else ... it had to happen. The music scene was so moribund at the time and it was so tediously boring that something had to happen, because we were people who didn't have a voice. People of late teens, early twenties, there was no way we were going to take any crap from the dinosaurs, the Rod Stewarts, the Yes's and the Emerson, Lake and Palmers of this world. Most definitely.

White Punks on Hope

Well, what should have been quite a punk rock event took place at Manchester's tacky (well not really) but small, Lesser Free Trade Hall recently. It wasn't as promising as it sounded, however. 'Sex Pistols' direct from their successful banning at 'The French European Punk Rock Festival', 'London's Rock Garden' and 'Dingwalls' were, as usual, on top punkish form.

FOTOS BY PAUL

Local punks 'Buzzcocks', coming over as a cross between 'Ramones' and 'Sex Pistols', supported admirably creating excitement and havoc onstage.

Those juvenile pooftahs 'Slaughter and the Dogs' completely ruined the whole affair. They proved, once and for all, that punk rockers they aint and came over as just a poor imitation of 'Flintlock' who are considerably less nauseating. Perhaps their parents could do us all a favour and just keep them indoors at nighttime.

Most of the capacity audience were there to see these kids perform. They were aged between about twelve and forty, probably their fan club. Anyway, when the 'Pistols' took the stage to perform some genuine punk rock, these people sensibly fled.

Let me say, at this point, that I had arranged to interview 'Sex Pistols' at this gig but unfortunately, Malcolm McLaren (the boss) said that the boys were too busy.

They crashed into 'Number One' the first number, and it was clear that they had improved musically since I last saw them (is nothing sacred?). Johnny Rotten still does an exquisite job in keeping it basic, yeah he's a hero. Their second number 'Pushin' and a Shovin'' is a minor classic. How can a bunch of

musical incompetents write stuff like this then? They have got talent and it's surfacing fast.

'I'm a Lazy Pseud' was next, followed by the fourth and fifth numbers. Musically they were just slowly improving and Johnny was the anchor, making certain that they didn't drift into anything too professional. The audience were still in their seats, prompting the band in between numbers.

"Substitute!", they shouted.

"You'll get it!", Johnny snarled. "Don't like impatience."

"No fun!", they continued.

"Well if you want fun why don't you start moving? You'll get piles up your backsides sitting in these seats like that" came Johnny's reply.

The next three numbers saw the audience starting to respond, the band continuing to improve and Johnny Rotten sounding and looking bored (he hates everything).

'No Feelings' is next, followed by 'No Fun'.

"Get fuckin' moving" Johnny shouts and the audience responds.

Johnny had already removed his red sweater and was down to his shirt and tie. He adjusted the tie and commenced to rip his shirt to shreds, an act that most of the audience decide to emulate. There are gonna be plenty of torn shirts as a result of this concert, it seems.

With practically everybody on their feet Johnny still shows his dissatisfaction.

"Some people never wake up. Got some statues here tonight", he leared. As usual, following 'No Fun' was 'Substitute', beats the shit out of the Who's original. The audience were wasted and the band were into 'I'm Pretty Vacant' without mercy. They just ploughed on sending the kids delirious. 'Problems' brought their set to a close and the audience went wild, bringing them back for an encore. 'I'm Goin Out of My Head (?)' was that final song which sent everybody home satisfied, and probably very tired. Sex Pistols cool O.K.

END

12

'How can a bunch of musical incompetents write tunes like this?'
Paul Welsh's glowing review of the second Pistols gig. © *Paul Welsh*

CHAPTER EIGHT

A GIRL OF ABOUT EIGHTEEN, WEARING GLASSES

When Oasis experienced their first rush of success, one wag coined a nickname for the inexplicably popular band from the perfectly pleasant south Manchester suburb of Burnage: the Sex Beatles. *Never Mind the Bollocks – Here's the Sex Pistols* is Noel Gallagher's joint favourite album of all time, along with the 'Blue' and 'Red' Beatles best-of compilations.

WAYNE BARRETT: I like Oasis. I'm sure they have the same kind of record collection as ours, apart from having a lot more Beatles than we did. But I like the characters of the two brothers. They show the talent, the 'aggressivity' of the Mancunian person. No Londoner or no Scotsman or Irishman or whatever could take that away from the

Mancunian. That's his sincerity – it might come out in a strange way but what he says is what he believes in.

And that just about sums up the way the events of 1976 in Manchester changed the shape of rock and a whole world of music. *Aggresivity*. Noel and Liam Gallagher would have been aged nine and four at the time – mere mono-browed tots – but, even after the fact, they got it. And thus became part of it.

TONY WILSON: The success of Manchester is in not being the typical city like Bristol, which has a good three years, or Seattle, which has a good three years, or Liverpool, which has a good three years. Manchester having a good twenty years begins that night on 4 June and it's as if you can use the phrase 'being set into motion'. The spin that was created that night lasted probably until Oasis.

MICK ROSSI: There's certain breeding you get being in Manchester. It's kind of in your blood, especially if you're into music. It just kind of crawls in, I think, naturally. I think Noel Gallagher is a genius – absolutely fantastic. I love Oasis.

TONY WILSON: Something about the energy imparted that night set up a train of events which takes us through to today. Factory Records would not have existed and my life would not have been what it was without Joy Division. And Joy Division got up on stage because they saw these buggers [Sex Pistols] on stage. Well, if they can do it, we can do it. That was the message.

The chain of events started on 4 June 1976 was to shape Manchester music. The city has always been the nation's tastemaker in terms of popular culture. For 'Manchester music', you can take it as read, in fact, that we are largely talking about 'British music'. In 1986 a music festival was held in Manchester marking a decade of influence following the Sex Pistols' performance at the Lesser Free Trade Hall. The climax of the 'Festival of the Tenth Summer' was a gig by The Fall, New Order and The Smiths, bands who were all links in the chain that drag us back to that lesser-spotted auditorium on Peter Street in Manchester.

JON THE POSTMAN: Well, they actually let the latent talent in people flourish, people who never would have actually got on stage, inspired by those gigs. It brought it out and there were actually a lot of talented people at those gigs. Mark E. Smith, Morrissey etc., etc., so would they have been inspired and actually done it if that hadn't occurred? I don't know – that's conjecture of course.

IAN MOSS: Much as I loved David Bowie and Roxy Music and Iggy Pop and Lou Reed, there was no way that I could have envisaged meeting those people or having anything to say to those people. With the Sex Pistols, all those barriers were down. Everybody was the same, you were as important as the band, right from the start it was obvious that the rock-star facade didn't exist. That was radical. Even the tinniest, most pathetic bands, the first thing they did probably before they learned to play was preening in a mirror and play at being a rock star. That was probably the most radical thing, to do away with that star system and all that nonsense; that idea that we are better than the audience.

In some quarters, to write, to care or even to think about rock music as anything other than a mild distraction is often sneered at. *It's Only Rock 'n' Roll*, after all. What a useless expression. Because, as the Sex Pistols' appearances at the Lesser Free Trade Hall show, rock music can actually change things. Granted, it tends to change items and areas of popular culture that have a direct link with it but it changes things nonetheless. Most importantly, it changes people. It can turn a shop worker into a writer, a council worker into a rock icon or TV presenter into a record mogul. And the people who were there, at the Lesser Free Trade Hall, definitely experienced a change.

PAUL MORLEY: The great thing about the Sex Pistols show was, physically and mentally, they were like us and they were doing something themselves. You thought, 'It can be done, you don't have to learn an instrument in that conventional way, you don't have to write in that conventional way'. They liberated you to be able to do it in a way that, for Britain and for me, was absolutely brand new. I always think of the great punk spirit being more like Surrealism or Dadaism. There's a tendency for people to look back on it and think of the gobbing and the safety pins. It was much more of an artistic kind of release and it was a continuation of Surrealism, rather than just giving you a chance to stick a safety pin through your cheek and gob on people.

PETE SHELLEY: I don't think it's just by chance that all these unknown people have gone to a gig and then, suddenly, all these people were all celebrated in one way or another. The chances of that happening, you know, choosing a random room. People must have felt, 'I can do that.'

IAN MOSS: Everything in Manchester that had any cultural significance, to this day, you can trace in some way back to the Sex Pistols playing at the Lesser Free Trade Hall. There would have been no Joy Division without the Sex Pistols. There would have been no Factory records, therefore no Haçienda. In Manchester's cultural heritage over the last forty years, that was the start of it. That made people go out and do things and believe that they could go out and do things and create things.

DAWN BRADBURY: No. Absolutely not. Why would you buy that? What it did was put the last big musical explosion on the map. The second gig, that is. The first gig was like a trailer you get in the cinema before the full film. The full event was the second gig. That was punk on the map in the north-west. Punk lasted 500 days. Start to finish, boom! Then gone. After that you get your new wave, your Adam Ant, your Duran Duran. Music becomes an adaptation, a regurgitation, a mash-up. If you were there and you experienced it – not just that one gig – but if you experienced that 500-day phenomena known as punk, that changed the person you would become. It had an impact on you as a person, on your beliefs, on your morals, on your ethics. We were very opinionated, very 'I'm going to say it as it is.' Very gung-ho really ... for a group of kids.

ALAN HEMPSALL: When I saw the Pistols, it took me a year until I joined a band. I wanted to be in a band but didn't have the discipline to learn an instrument. Be a singer – that would be easier. I met up with these people and, unfortunately, none of them had seen the Pistols. They were very much 'old school' with the long hair and the 'let's have guitar solos'. I actually got fired after three months because I couldn't sing. So I decided, if I formed my own band, I couldn't get fired.

TONY WILSON: Whenever you see a band and you've got that look in the seventeen-year-olds' eyes, that they're not on that stage because they want to be pop stars, they want to make music. They're on stage because they have no fucking choice, which is what all great bands look like, be that the Pistols or Joy Division.

We may have left it a little late into the proceedings for this, but I'm afraid I wasn't there. At twelve, I was a few years too young. But I've always been fascinated by the idea of being in places at a time when, in the years ahead, people would actually be interested to hear your recollections; that your very presence becomes part of the narrative.

And this is where my interest in that narrative comes from: when I first started work on a magazine in 1981, aged sixteen, a photographer in his twenties named Peter Oldham was assigned to look after me. He had a blood-red fuel-injected Ford and used to flick his wrist when changing gears as he drove. Impossibly swish. To pass the time as we travelled to cheque presentations and Golden Wedding celebrations, we would talk about music, especially punk rock. Peter told me he had been to both of the Sex Pistols' gigs at the Lesser Free Trade Hall five years earlier.

By this stage – just five years after the summer of 1976 – half of the city was claiming to have attended, so I took Peter's claim with a generous handful of salt. He then produced his ticket and the photos he took from the stalls with his trusty Zenith to prove his point. '*Bastard*', I thought. Peter made copies of his pictures and I have kept them ever since, always wanting to get to the truth behind the story. Peter is, I suspect, slightly baffled by the way I've held a torch for this for so long. It's because it *matters* ... it matters that the date on the ticket was wrong, that Buzzcocks were replaced by Howard's mate Geoff's progressive-rock band, that Shelley and Devoto nearly got a good hiding to keep them off the bill at the second gig and it matters that we now know who Gentlemen are. The problem is, I just don't know why it matters. It just does, OK?

To those who understand this, detail and facts count for a great deal. Who, what, when, where, why are paramount. But these things can get complicated – time and reinvention can muddy the waters.

If I am ever asked the 'What was the first gig you ever went to?' question, the reply I give is always delivered as quick as a shot, without hesitation, with a slight flourish: XTC – 'Manchester Polytechnic All Saints' Building, April 1978.' And every time it happens, I inwardly release a little shot of guilt into myself. Not enough to double myself up, just sufficient to provide a twinge. Because, in my heart of hearts, I actually know it was 1979. Very early 1979, mind you. Don't get me wrong. It's just that 1978 sounds so much better. I believe that this is a fairly common problem. I suppose it's because 1978 is a step closer to 1977. Which is a step closer still to 1976. Or 1076, if you're to believe the hand-printed lettering on the ticket of that first Pistols' gig at the Lesser Free Trade Hall.

In April 1979 I had just turned my hair bleach-blond. On the night of my first gig I had PVC trousers on as I waited outside the Polytechnic to see XTC. I stood on tiptoes inside my zip-up boots to make myself appear taller and thus improve my chances of getting in ... because it was an over-eighteens venue and I was barely fourteen. After I did get in, I only have three memories of the entire event. I can remember that the wall behind the stage had a mural of Dennis the Menace and Gnasher on it. I can remember that, at one stage, a skinhead pushed lead singer Andy Partridge away from the microphone and took over vocal duties himself. And I can remember that a girl of about eighteen, wearing glasses, allowed me to hold her jumper-covered breasts from behind during the encores. Oh yes ... and I remember being sick the whole of the following day because of the amount of alcohol I had consumed. About three and a half pints of bitter. Despite this, for years I genuinely believed that beer tasted best drunk from a plastic pint-pot. The kind they serve at gigs.

Not a groundbreaking event, you might say. They're unlikely to make a documentary or publish a book about that, you might add. I hear what you're saying. But still, not bad for a fourteen-year-old from Altrincham at his first ever gig. What can I say, you know ... that's what 1978 was like.

Sorry. 1979.

The reason I bring it up is because the other thing that has always fascinated me is people's desire to have been 'there'. Wherever or whenever 'there' happens to be . That moment that the world shifts just enough to make a difference. If the presence of truth doesn't actually match our desire for it, a little sleight of hand can be brought into play. Have you ever invited someone round to your house and placed your better, smarter, cooler records to the front of the pile before they have arrived? Ever written the name of a band on your satchel, only to scrub it off when you spy another kid with the same name on their schoolbag? Ever forced yourself to listen to Captain Beefheart's *Trout Mask Replica* while quietly coveting your sister's Jackson 5 album? Then you know what I mean. There are lots of reasons why anyone might wish to say, 'I Swear I Was There'.

PHIL SINGLETON: It made a fantastic story for everybody involved – it's worthwhile for them, whether it's the Sex Pistols, whether it's Tony Wilson, whether it's Granada because of *So It Goes*, and it ties in with the Manchester music scene being shaken up. Nothing is as straightforward as that, a lot of chance is involved, a lot of luck involved, there's a lot of hindsight involved. It's like a lot of the stories about punk rock – it's now a given that this happened and it's bolted down. This is one segment of rock that is a fact and it's in its box and that's it. Very few people would be willing to sit down and pick through that box and take it apart.

JOHN BERRY: Everyone rewrites their history. Everyone embellishes. Everyone wants to be something they're not. It was a lot easier to 'be there' then because there was so little photographic evidence. We didn't have cameras. No one that I ever went to a concert with ever had a camera. I can kind of understand it because it's a damn sight easier to do now.

The stories surrounding the three events described here – the first and second gigs at the Lesser Free Trade Hall and the Pistols' performance on *So It Goes* – are touched upon in every book about the Sex Pistols and British punk rock ever written. The same stories are trotted out but rarely is anyone who was actually there actually asked what really happened. Print the myth, not the truth. When you do ask, it becomes like the fable of the blind men feeling an elephant ... each coming up with a totally different impression from their contact with a slightly different part of the animal.

JOHN MAHER: As you know, you ask a hundred people, you get a hundred different versions. The danger with the way some things are being documented, there becomes an official version. Other people then regurgitate it and then that becomes 'how it was' for everybody. I hear people telling me what it was like back then, people who were about three years old at the time. They clearly didn't experience it but, in their heads, they have, because they've had this thing fed to them so often.

In 2011 the *NME* – the paper that printed the story in 1976 that drew Pete Shelley and Howard Devoto to London to see the Pistols – produced a special edition about the hundred most important gigs of all time. From Oasis at Main Road, Manchester in 1996, via Queen at Live Aid in 1985, to David Bowie sending Ziggy Stardust into retirement at the Hammersmith Odeon in 1973 – all the gigs you should have been to were listed. At Number One was the Sex Pistols – plus support from Solstice, lest we forget – at the Lesser Free Trade Hall on 4 June 1976. A garage band, playing a few cover versions and a smattering of their own tunes, in front of a few dozen long-hairs in a seated auditorium in Manchester was named as the most important gig of all time. I was asked to provide a rundown of who I thought was or was not there and Paul Morley weighed in with his thoughts: 'Rotten made us believe in the dark menacing fairytale of punk, and the rest was post-punk history.'

TONY WILSON: If you talk to Mark E. Smith, talk to Hooky [Peter Hook] or Barney [Bernard Sumner], or any of them, it was all like, Oh my God, the Pistols were fantastic because (a) it *was* fantastic and (b) they just got on stage. So the idea that you needed to be special or you needed to have five-thousand pounds' worth of synthesisers and being Rick Wakeman or needing a music degree – all that bollocks – was just removed, got rid of.

PETER HOOK: The thing that shapes Manchester music is ... Manchester. To my mind, we actually did it better than they did. Manchester is a fantastic musical place and sometimes, when I look back at how many bands have come out of Manchester and how important they are, it's just unbelievable.

TONY WILSON: When Manchester celebrated the dawn of the millennium, after the fanfare at midnight, the first minute of 2000, what song did they play? In the main arena, to the 10,000 people dancing up and down, they played 'Hey Jude'. In Manchester. Doesn't mean you've got to be stupid, right? The Beatles from Liverpool, The Rolling Stones from London. Doesn't matter where it comes from. Doesn't matter that the Pistols were London, that's not important. We played our part – they played their part. It's a wonderful, wonderful world.

One question that I put to Tony Wilson was put to all the interviewees: 'Are we over-exaggerating this in terms of importance? Are we just shitting this up into something it isn't?' Interestingly, one of the few dissenting voices was former Sex Pistol Glen Matlock. And we know he was *definitely* there.

GLEN MATLOCK: What, the good old days and all that? Well, a bit of that ... I think there was a sea change, but I don't think that was because of we did then ... I think people were looking for stuff.

Which, put another way ... it's not so much that the Pistols were so fantastic; it is that the alternatives available at the time were so deeply *unfantastic*. And that made the band seem impossibly attractive, glamorous even. I do believe that people like the idea of the Sex Pistols considerably more than they do the reality – happier to wear a logoed T-shirt or wield an ironic tea mug, rather than actually listen to *Never Mind The Bollocks*. More likely, the attraction lies in the fact that the name 'Sex Pistols' still carries a shudder-value with it, even after all this time. Yet the source of their notoriety – having a cheeky name, wearing unusual clothes and swearing a bit on the television – is pretty small beer compared to what we expect of bands today. Yet these modern bands are seen as panto acts; a bit of fun. In 1976 the Pistols seemed like a genuine threat to society, merely because everything else was so unthreatening. The notoriety they generated was whistles and bells – a distraction from the real thing: four lads playing rock 'n' roll just that little bit harder, faster and hungrier than anyone around them. And wearing the right trousers, of course.

Which is all that Slaughter And The Dogs were trying to do. Slaughter have taken a lot of stick over the years, mainly because of the 'glam' thing. Yes, it's true – both Wayne Barrett and Mick Rossi were wearing what can only be described as 'blouses' for the second gig. And, yes, their bass player Howard Bates had hair that stretched down to the bottom of his rib cage. But that makes them no different to a hundred other bands that headed for the barbers in the wake of punk rock. If anything, they were earlier than most.

Punk is an easy word to throw around. It sticks to a lot of cultural flypaper, most of the time inappropriately. But it's down to the beholder: the kid in Baltimore with Nirvana, Green Day and My Chemical Romance on shuffle play knows exactly what it means. So does the fifty-something Stiff Little Fingers fan in Anytown, UK, preparing to push his mates around to 'Alternative Ulster' at their local civic centre. To cover that amount of ground, punk must have made an awful lot of connections to many, many people. But punk, we are told, was over by the end of 1976. The rope was quietly hooked over the entrance to the VIP area, barring entry to anyone who hadn't stepped inside by the time Steve Jones was calling Bill Grundy a 'fucking rotter'.

PHIL SINGLETON: If you're involved in it and you claim to be at the very start of something, once it becomes well-liked by other people, once the genie is out, those that were in at the beginning disown it and say, 'It's over - punk is dead.' Have they the right to say that? For everybody else, beyond their little group, then the answer has to be no. They have no right to say that punk is now dead, just because everyone knows about it. But we all feel that way, if you're into a group and there's only a few of your mates into them. Pity the poor Adam And The Ants fans when they were cool, hardcore punk. Suddenly you find little Johnny at primary school down the road with toothpaste across his nose. That must be so heartbreaking.

But what other movement of youth and music other than punk is still a badge to be worn proudly, more than forty years after it began? What other slice of popular culture is still being embraced by little Johnnys – and embossed on their T-shirts – in countries across the world? Punk, it seems, far from being over in December 1976, has outlived them all. What we need now is a reason. Plus, of course, a dissenting voice.

HOWARD DEVOTO: I think, as it transpired, that the immediacy of being in a punk group – the whole thing of,

'Well, we can hardly play, but here we are on stage and we're writing this song as we're playing it, and it's going to be over in thirty seconds!' That was setting yourself off against the kinds of things you'd be seeing in pubs, which would either be earnest folk-rock stuff or prog-rock stuff, where people were trying to be flash and heavy with as much heavy equipment as they could manage. Punk did try and take over all aspects of music ... where you played, how your records looked, the whole thing of suddenly everybody had to have a picture disc, the way people looked, the way they related to the music business, the kind of music they played. One attempted to try and change everything.

TONY WILSON: There is a bit of cultural theory from my dear guitarist, Vini Reilly [Durutti Column – he was also briefly in Ed Banger And The Nosebleeds] to explain punk and the development of the Pistols. Punk not only changed culture, it actually radicalised music in terms of melody, chords, and modality. We hippie kids from the 1960s and early 1970s, we learned the guitar and you learn chords that play the one, four, five, tonal development which is what twentieth century Western music is based around. You learn C ... F ... G7 [fingers imaginary chords]. If you couldn't play guitar at all, you'd just play an F chord, an F shape. Suddenly, if you can't play at all, and you're doing this bar chord, you go up and down. You watch any punk band [slides hand up and down imaginary guitar neck]. So, suddenly, melody was freed from the constraints of the previous twenty years – that is why it freed melody and allowed new melodic things to happen and why it sounded so fresh. That's not me, that's Vini my guitarist telling me that.

JORDAN: I think the most important part of it is [that] it empowered the youth of that time to do their own thing. It sounds kind of corny to say, 'to rebel against their parents.' They felt a camaraderie, if you like. People were drawn together in big gangs, but not necessarily aggressive gangs. The press wanted to make it out that it was much like the mods and rockers. They tried to incite violence between, say, the skinheads and punks, because they didn't want it all to be peaceful and happy. The youth were empowered to be their own man or woman – and that's another thing as well: the sexes weren't quite so separated during that time. You wouldn't see girls going to clubs dressing up just to please men. They dressed up to please themselves and in a way it was a sort of sexual revolution, because nobody was playing games with anybody. You dressed up to look great whether you were a man or a woman and there was no role-playing.

WILL BIRCH (author: *No Sleep Till Canvey Island – The Great Pub Rock Revolution*): I don't think the Sex Pistols were musically of any interest at all. I think the lyrics were tremendous and I think Johnny Rotten's vocal style was great, hugely entertaining. I think the whole Sex Pistols image and the way they launched themselves in London was outrageous, so fantastic. But as far as the music was concerned – I don't want to come across as a muso, because I hope I'm not a muso – their actual backing was really bog standard. There was nothing new about it at all. But I think they were about the only one of those punk-rock groups of the early half-dozen or so big names that did that kind of 'pushing against the beat' thing that the Stones or the Faces would do. That was tremendously old-fashioned. They did that and they got away with it. The Clash would never do that, or The Ramones or Buzzcocks.

STEVE DIGGLE: It did change the world in its way. I think it gave you a confidence and it gave you a way of questioning things. It gave you a bravery. All those people in the audience, unsung kids, punk-rock warriors – they were the foot soldiers. Then suddenly this junta came together, trying to control it ... Tony Wilson and [music writer] Jon Savage ... Who the fuck are they to control it? It was in the hands of the kids. That's what made it: the kids who bought the records, the kids we spoke to. Foot soldiers, y'know? The Kids.

The achievements of Buzzcocks are extraordinary, not only in their organisation of both gigs but in their production of *Spiral Scratch*, the first independent record produced by a 'punk' band. To hear Pete Shelley speak about these events, he could almost be addressing a motivational business seminar – albeit in a very soft voice.

PETE SHELLEY: It seemed an impossible dream. We didn't realise it was as simple as just doing it. Lots of people realised they could do it. People were saying, 'I'm a writer.' Instead of people saying, 'No, you're not,' they believed them and let them get on with writing.

STEVE DIGGLE: May I say that first, it changed us and then we changed Manchester. Bands like The Fall saw what Buzzcocks were doing 'cause we let them support us. John Cooper Clarke supported us. Joy Division? Bernard Sumner came to this shop looking for a guitar with us – they didn't even have a name then. Buzzcocks changed Manchester. The Sex Pistols started off on a more cosmopolitan level coming from London, but we made the provinces cool. First of all it happened in Manchester and then six months later you had places like Liverpool and Sheffield happening.

The story of the Pistols' first appearance on television on *So It Goes* shows how a triumphant moment in pop-culture history can get snatched from the jaws of chaos. It's remarkable that Glen Matlock was not even aware that there were other bands on the programme. Having said that, they were ensconced in a dressing room arguing about Jordan's armband at the time. The following series of *So It Goes* changed out of all recognition from the pseudo-comedy show that the Pistols found themselves on. It provided not only a record of bands like The Clash, Penetration and Siouxsie And The Banshees but laid the groundwork for a music-television format that would be picked up by nearly every music show since.

For the purposes of this book, I took Glen Matlock into Studio Two at Granada Television in Manchester – the studio where he made his first television appearance in 1976. 'Yeah,' he said. 'I remember this. There was seats over there...' He then recalled calling Tony Wilson a cunt.

GLEN MATLOCK: To me, music is communicating with people. Music is picking up a guitar and playing in front of somebody and getting some feedback straight away. I'm not a Luddite, I've got a computer at home and all that; I can do all that. What you choose to do with it is another matter, but it's so laborious and it's so slow. It's a joke. With a guitar you go 'deh deh...' and something's happening straight away – it's more immediate. That's why I like it. If you don't relate to people, it's just wanking.

So the events in Manchester in the summer of 1976 were a lot of things. Inspiring? Obviously. Iconic? Definitely. Clouded by mists and mirrors as to what the truth about them really was? Totally. As Pete Shelley says, 'There's a lot of unanswered questions about those gigs – might have been something in the beer...'

HOWARD DEVOTO: I know that it changed my life beyond a whole roomful of shadows of doubt – forever.

The main thing – and the reason that it's really important – is that it's such a *strange* tale: the kind that leads to an inevitable myth. Two young guys see an article, travel to London, organise a gig and that gig changes the world of music. Then lots of people say, *I Swear I Was There*.

It's important because, if nothing else, it's a great story.

The innocuous, scribbled diary entry heralding the gig that changed the world. © *Manchester Libraries Information and Archive*

CHAPTER NINE

A MARVELLOUS JOB IN SHIPPING

Much has happened to our cast of players in the forty years since the Sex Pistols took to the stage of the Lesser Free Trade Hall. The Pistols themselves technically split after their show at the Winterland Ballroom in San Francisco in January 1978, at the end of a seven-date tour of entirely inappropriate cities and venues in the American South.

Glen Matlock had 'left' the group by that stage, to be replaced by Sid Vicious, who died in February 1978 in a heroin haze of mystery after his girlfriend Nancy Spungen was found stabbed in their hotel room in New York.

John Lydon's post-Pistols career continued as leader of Public Image Limited and his rarely mentioned, but not unreasonable, attempts at acting, such as his film debut in *Order Of Death* in 1983. Then, eighteen years after the

Winterland split, the original Pistols reformed to play gigs in Europe, America, Australia, New Zealand, Japan and South America. In 2002, spurred on, no doubt, by the hilarious 'Jubilee' possibilities, the band reformed again to play Crystal Palace Sports Arena on 27 July, missing the Queen's Golden Jubilee by nearly seven weeks. John Lydon has since declared it was his favourite ever Pistols gig. The following year he accepted the invitation of Granada Television (which had, after all, put him into our front rooms for the first time ever in 1976 on *So It Goes*) to appear on the reality jungle quest *I'm A Celebrity ... Get Me Out of Here*. In accepting the invite, he managed to lose his status as a potential winner of the series by walking off the show. But not before tussling with ostriches, kicking the odd camera and charming the nation with his enthusiasm for wildlife and the insect world in particular. And calling the viewing audience 'cunts' on live television. He is now a chat-show regular, enthusiastic butter salesman, wildlife presenter and continuing frontman for Public Image and, when it suits him, the Sex Pistols.

After a slightly under-achieving career in a music – including a stint as lead singer with The Professionals alongside Pistols drummer Paul Cook – guitarist Steve Jones now presents 'Jonesy's Jukebox' radio show on 95.5 KLOSFM in Los Angeles. In 2015 he celebrated twenty five years of being drink-and-drug free. Pistols drummer Paul Cook plays in the side-group Manraze with Simon Laffy and Phil Collen, both formerly of early 1980s glam-metal act Girl, though Collen is better known as guitarist in rockers

Def Leppard. He played with a reformed Professionals – minus Steve Jones – in 2015.

Glen Matlock formed Rich Kids in 1977 with Steve New and Rusty Egan. Midge Ure joined shortly afterwards and they spent five weeks in the charts the following year with their eponymous power-pop anthem 'Rich Kids'. They made one album, *Ghosts Of Princes In Towers*, and managed the difficult, three-way trick of being in at the start of 'New Wave', prefiguring much of the mist-shrouded imagery of the New Romantics ... and not being very successful.

GLEN MATLOCK: It's the way of the rock business. At the time, I think Rich Kids paved the way for lots of other bands – the Skids, people like The Eurythmics. Even those girls who ended up doing 'Don't You Want Me Baby' [Susanne Sulley and Joanne Catherall of The Human League], they were down the front of our gigs. The rock business is never a big sea change – there's always a little bit of this and a little bit of that. It kind of teeters forward from one thing to the next.

He's since worked with the late Jackie Leven, former lead singer with Scottish new-wave/folk nutcases Doll By Doll, and toured with his band The Philistines. They released their debut album, called *Open Mind* in 2000, which got healthy reviews.

GLEN MATLOCK: Is that surprising? People think that you do something and then you just totally forget how to do anything associated with it. But songwriting is a craft and you learn and hone as you get a bit older. I try to keep my ear to the ground and finger on the pulse of what's going on. Whether you choose to do that or not – follow the trend – I personally choose not to. Other people do that. I think I'm as contemporary as the next bloke but it's just people's perceptions. People actually like what I'm doing. I've written some good songs in the past and I will continue to write songs, so you shouldn't be so surprised.

Today, Matlock cuts a trim, geezer-ish figure whose cor-blimey voice and tendency to wear daytime shades distract from him being an ordinary bloke who's lived through extraordinary times. Matlock was the youngest Pistol but only by a matter of months. Today he looks years younger than the others. A female colleague who sat in during our talk described him as 'the only actually sexy Pistol'. He's played with Dead Men Walking, a rolling-revue project which features a variable cast that can feature Pete Wylie (The Mighty Wah!), Mike Peters (The Alarm), Kirk Brandon (Theatre of Hate) or Slim Jim Phanton (Stray Cats). The ever-changing membership play each other's songs and tell stories. It's a sort of post-punk *Vagina Monologues*. He's also played with punky 'supergroups' The Flying Padovanis and Slinky Vagabound, as well as a reformed version of the Faces. In 2010, when original Faces singer Rod Stewart dropped out of a reunion show after the band was inducted into the Rock And Roll Hall Of Fame, his place was taken by none other than Mick Hucknall. Of all the Pistol's, Matlock has remained the busiest.

GLEN MATLOCK: What do you do – crawl under a stone, just 'cause it suits everybody else? Fuck that. I've come to the conclusion that you can't please everybody, so you might as well please yourself. I keep writing all the time anyway and I've got sackfuls and sackfuls of songs. I mean, some of them are cobblers but some of them are good. So there's no point in them being in a cassette in your bottom drawer.

Howard Devoto now lives in east London and, for some years, worked as a photo-archive director. With his close-cropped hair and heavy black spectacles, he looks a little like a cross between new-wave singer Joe Jackson and ex-footballer Nobby Stiles – only with a degree in Humanities. Far from his enigmatic image, he is keen and able to talk about the events of 1976 and beyond. The band he formed when he left Buzzcocks – Magazine – were probably the purest statement of post-punk. They took the edge but left behind the posturing. They kept the distorted guitars but overlaid them with clean keyboard lines. They predicted both the cold detachment of the New Romantics and the psychedelic swirl of the Liverpool groups that would dominate the early 1980s: Echo And The Bunnymen and The Teardrop Explodes. They were way ahead of their time but, listening to their key track, 'Shot By Both Sides', it's striking how much the main, ascending riff sounds like

Mountain's 'Nantucket Sleighride', as played by Lesser Free Trade Hall-favourites Solstice.

Magazine reformed in 2009, playing shows in Manchester, Edinburgh and London. The group also acted as an extraordinary 'Job Centre' for other bands to poach personnel from and created even more complex connections to the Sex Pistols than that night in June at the Lesser Free Trade Hall: Magazine guitarist John McGeogh went on to join Siouxsie and the Banshees; Sid Vicious was an early member of the Banshees; Vicious, of course, replaced Glen Matlock in the Pistols in February 1977; McGeogh later joined Public Image Limited with John Lydon; Magazine bass player Barry Adamson and keyboardist Dave Formula joined Steve Strange's Visage project, which also included Midge Ure, who'd previously been in Rich Kids with Glen Matlock. Incestuous times. Howard and Pete came together again in 2001 under the banner of ShelleyDevoto, releasing an album called *Buzzcunst* the following year.

HOWARD DEVOTO: In some kind of curious turn of events, Pete Shelley and myself found ourselves working together again. There's computers – you don't sit around with a guitar anymore in your front room. You still sit around in your front room, but it's with a computer more than a guitar. It's was actually fantastic to work with him again. He and I have not really worked together since 1977, sometime after *Spiral Scratch* and I'd left the band. We hadn't even particularly seen that much of each other, maybe once every two or three years. Suddenly, we were seeing each other every week. It was great to be getting to know him again but, more than that, I really liked the music we're doing.

PETE SHELLEY: It was really good working with Howard because, in some ways, I'd forgotten about how mad he was in the first place. At the start of Buzzcocks, you always think of Howard as being very enigmatic. But really, he's as mad as a brush!

HOWARD DEVOTO: *Buzzkunst* didn't sound to me like what either of us have done quite before. That there was a kind of aggression to it, that's still important to me. Do people understand that word 'edge' anymore? I don't, awful word ... let's talk about resonance. No, definitely don't talk about resonance. Hell, I don't know, I mean it ain't punk rock, I'll tell you that. Well, apart from a little bit. A little bit of it's punk rock – about one seventeenth of it is punk rock.

When Pete Shelley continued with Buzzcocks after Devoto's departure, he and Diggle created a body of albums – and particularly singles – that generated hits and affection in equal measure. The game of spot-the-Buzzcocks-influence is as easy today as it's ever been. Bands from Blink 182 to Green Day and Nirvana – as well as lovelorn emo stars like Fall Out Boy and My Chemical Romance – all owe Buzzcocks a debt of inspiration. So does any band that has set up their own record label to bypass the system and release their own product. By 1981 Buzzcocks had split, only to reform by the end of the decade, with a full-on comeback in 1993 with the album *Trade Test Transmissions*. In between, Shelley worked with The Invisible Girls and released material under the heading of The Tiller Boys. As a solo artist, his 1982 album *Homosapien* was a well-received slice of electro-pop that was completely of its time. He still records and tours with Buzzccocks, all these years after events at the Lesser Free Trade Hall.

PETE SHELLEY: Even though I was twenty one when it all happened, it seems a long time ago, but strangely quite recent.

In 2009 Shelley and Devoto were awarded honorary doctorates from the University Of Bolton in recognition of their contribution to music. They were, according to vice-chancellor Dr George Holmes, 'examples of the shining talent within the Bolton family.' *Family Fortunes* presenter Vernon Kay got one too.

Steve Diggle now lives in London. Not looking particularly different from the way he did in the 1970s, he will happily mock his fellow Buzzcocks' lack of hair while casually ruffling his own dark locks. 'Can't go bald in this game,' he told me. 'It's a rock 'n' roll war crime, that is...' As well as his Buzzcocks output, his own band, Flag Of Convenience, and solo projects, including a solo album in 2005 called *Serious Contender*, his taste for champagne – 'rock 'n' roll mouthwash' – has helped a phrase enter the lexicon of touring groups everywhere. A phrase from the rider statement of what is required for the band backstage...

STEVE DIGGLE: Yeah, 'No Moet, No Show-ay, No Chandon, No Band On.' When you were younger, you'd have six or seven pints of beer before you went on. As you get older, you're still jumping around, but the beer gets a bit heavy. Plus there's not always time to have the six or seven pints that's required. So we got into the champagne. I don't play golf and I don't have any hobbies, but I drink the champagne 'cause it's rock 'n' roll fuel and it gets you in the mood quick. It wasn't a statement. I think the catchphrase caught on with these heavy metal bands.

Buzzcocks' drummer John Maher – just sixteen when he played his first ever gig at the Lesser Free Trade Hall – now lives on Harris in the Outer Hebrides. As well as his business involving high-performance Volkswagen engines, he's also a respected photographer.

JOHN MAHER: The photography? It's like anything else in my so-called adult life: a hobby that turns into a job. Something that you like that ends up gaining more notoriety than you thought it would. It's a great place for photography. The quality of light up here is amazing.

When Buzzcocks split in 1981, Maher worked with Pauline Murray of Penetration, Steve Diggle's Flag Of Convenience and Pete Wylie's WAH! He left the music industry after rejoining Buzzcocks in 1989. In 2012 he returned to the Buzzcocks' fold to recreate the Lesser Free Trade Hall line-up of the band – and their post-Devoto pop heyday – for two special gigs in Manchester and London. The gigs also saw Howard Devoto return to the band for the first time since he quit in 1977. Not everyone came away from the gigs entirely happy with what had happened, not least John Maher.

JOHN MAHER: It was weird. There was a bit of aggro over Howard's fee. It spoiled it for me. It became about money and not about the music. He only came on for four songs. Steve made it quite clear from his body language that he didn't approve. [During the Manchester show, Diggle sat down during part of Devoto's appearance, stopped playing to take a drink and blew Devoto a kiss as he left the stage. At the end of the gig he told the crowd, 'We'll be back next time with the proper fucking band.'] Steve didn't do a great job on those two nights. I just wish he'd shown the other people on stage with him a bit more respect than he did. I grafted away for five months to get myself in shape for those gigs. I wanted to do as good a job as I could. If I had my time over again and they said, 'Would you come and do it...?' I'd say no. A lot of people enjoyed it but it didn't really represent what I liked about Buzzcocks. Things have come full circle though, I've done some live dates and an album with Penetration, so the drum kit's been out as well.

After a riotous 1980s, Tony Wilson came back down to earth with a bump. Factory Communications went bankrupt on

24 November 1992 with debts of more than £2 million. Rather inconveniently, the 24th was a Tuesday, denying headline writers their 'UNHAPPY MONDAY splash by twenty four hours. Speaking to reporters outside Factory's offices, Wilson tried to ride out the crash in a typically Wilsonesque fashion, blaming, of all things, a lack of restraint.

TONY WILSON: Factory tried to do too many things, from adventurous buildings to ambitious recording projects, at a time when signs of a negative economic climate ahead suggested restraint. Our principal sadness is for the people we've had to lay off. We regret the failure of our efforts to survive this crisis intact.

The final jewel in Wilson's crown, The Haçienda, would limp on for another five years. Despite a final giddy flush where attendances were back on the up, the former boat showroom in central Manchester that briefly became one of the world's most famous nightclubs closed its doors for the last time in June 1997. It had survived the notoriety of being associated with the UK's first ecstasy-related death and becoming the accidental flashpoint for rival-gang activity; in fact, the club was killed off by nothing more sinister than competition from other venues across Manchester and the north of England – the very venues it had inspired.

After a return to searching for teenagers with 'that look in their eyes' via the Factory Too and F4 labels, Wilson came back to television presenting in 2001. He fronted programmes for Granada Television such as *Soccer Brain*

The Sport Exchange and even returned to reading Granada's regional news presenting *Granada Reports*. Wilson left Granada again in 2003 after rather fantastically saying 'fucking' during an afternoon news bulletin. He pursued politics via an attempt to launch a north-west parliament and maintained his musical profile via the In The City showcase and convention held annually in Manchester, and broadcasting on XFM. In 2002 the film of Wilson's life and times, *24 Hour Party People*, was released. Directed by Michael Winterbottom, the film's first key scene is Wilson, played by Steve Coogan, at the Lesser Free Trade Hall on 4 June 4 1976, watching the Sex Pistols. It was filmed in the lesser-spotted auditorium itself, while it was unoccupied and derelict. I interviewed Wilson at the time for the original *I Swear I Was There* and he held forth on the subject of his attendance at the first Pistols' gig, despite all the evidence to the contrary.

TONY WILSON: In the original film screenplay it was like everyone pogoing and jumping up and down and it was a riot. A lot of the movie's not real – you can be unreal. But the reality is, there was no pogoing. Pogo really hadn't been invented at that point. The people who were there were just sitting, sitting in these chairs just ... gobsmacked. I became involved and thought it was a good idea. It's like a *Boogie Nights* concept. The dawn of punk to the death of acid, taking you through two revolutions on their up and down cycles. The film has resolved itself into being not really about the music; it's more a comedy about a bunch of idiots, which is me and my mates. A black comedy because quite a few people die in it.

Tony Wilson died on 10 August 2007. Cancer. The critical success of *24 Hour Party People* had dragged Wilson out of the wilderness and he was back on the radio and TV with the BBC and had just started presenting a new music show on Manchester's Channel M. He carried on presenting the BBC's *Sunday Politics* show, despite being visibly, desperately ill. For decades, Wilson had put up with shouted abuse on the streets of Manchester: 'Oi Wilson, ya fookin' wanker!' During his illness, he was able to return the favour. When people would approach him and ask after his health, Wilson would sometimes tell them to 'fucking fuck off'.

After his death, Wilson was proclaimed as 'The Man They Called Mr Manchester', despite the fact that no one had ever referred to him as Mr Manchester. Ever. During his time at Granada, I had shared an open-plan office with Wilson. He helped get the original *I Swear I Was There* documentary off the ground and it was his idea to include *So It Goes* in the story – the 'three great events of the summer of 1976', as he described the Lesser Free Trade Hall gigs and the Pistols' first TV appearance. Despite this, I didn't care for him – he represented the 'old guard'. Work tended to grind to a halt when he was around and he seemed vain and theatrical. Not only this, he caused me problems. As well as being a programme maker, I was head of the journalists' union at Granada – the NUJ Father of the Chapel, as it's known – and the 'saying-fuck-during-the-news-incident' occurred on my watch. He once invited me onto one of his radio shows to talk about the Pistols at the Lesser Free Trade Hall. During a break for traffic and weather, he leaned in and, in a rather threatening manner, pulled me up for suggesting he hadn't attended the first gig. When I tried to explain that it wasn't me who was suggesting it, it was virtually everyone I'd interviewed, he shoved up the fader and carried on with the show as if nothing had happened.

In 2008, with the blessing of his partner, Yvette Livesey, I wrote Tony's biography, *You're Entitled To An Opinion*. I spoke to scores of people, including one of his old school friends, who told me that Tony used to organise concerts in his teens. Wilson would never actually take part in these events – his job was to convince everyone that the performance was going to be the greatest thing ever and that you would be an idiot to miss it. It made me realise the importance of Wilson's role in the Manchester music scene: he was the ballyhoo man, the roll-up-roll-up barker outside the tent, tempting people to try Manchester's wares. The narrative of 'everything started with the Pistols coming to Manchester' was his invention. It didn't matter if he was there or not, because it had *worked*. By the time the book was published, I had learned to like Tony Wilson a great deal.

One of the other main characters in the *24 Hour Party People* film was Hooky – Peter Hook. The man who learned how to play bass guitar after seeing the Pistols was played by actor Ralf Little, Anthony in the BBC's *The Royle Family*, written by Hook's ex-wife Caroline Aherne. After recording one album under the name Revenge, Hook formed Monaco with tape operator David Potts. Hook was there when New Order returned in 1998, recording two albums before his relationship with former school friend and fellow Lesser Free Trade Hall alumni Bernard Sumner finally fractured in 2007. Despite howls of protest from Hook fans, Sumner and New Order carried on without him, recording a Hook-less album, *Music Complete*, in 2015. Hook now tours and records Joy Division and New Order material as Peter Hook And The Light. Of all those who can say 'I Swear I Was There', Hook – the beeriest of the Joy Division beer boys – is probably the most vocal about it.

PETER HOOK: See...I can prove I was there. I know all these *truths*.

The one band never featured in *24 Hour Party People* was the band that was airbrushed out of history. Bolton's Solstice turned to the safer waters of the cabaret circuit shortly after supporting the Sex Pistols in 1976. They carried on playing 'Night Fever' and 'Play That Funky Music, White Boy' until fizzling out in 1979. Guitarist Geoff Wild moved to South Africa, where he continued as a professional musician. Bassist Paul Flintoff and drummer Harry Box went on to work in the lighting industry. Singer Kimble lives locally and is described by the others as merely 'a character'. The three members of the Solstice co-operative I managed to track down agreed to meet me in a moorland pub on the outskirts of Darwen in Lancashire. Equal parts bemused and surprised at being traced, they are rightly proud of the following they had and the professionalism with which they generated and maintained it. Plus, they played at one of the most important gigs of all time. Although a similar age to the Pistols and a damn site younger than many 'converts', they never jumped on the punk bandwagon.

NEAL HOLDEN (lighting – Solstice): The reason the band dressed in white was because it looked good with the lights. The lights wouldn't work with short hair and black gear. That's why we did what we did. We didn't like punk. I did toy with the idea of doing a punk set. It could have made money. We were watching the punk bands doing really well but we never liked the material. Plus, the gigs that they did were bloody frightening. We did record some stuff. I ended up going down to London, to Wardour Street. I went to Polydor, Parlophone, Rocket Records ... taking a tape around. It didn't get us anywhere.

DAVE EYRE (soundman – Solstice): We just didn't like it. Neal tried to force us to change but we didn't like it.

DAWN BRADBURY: It wasn't their bag. Not at all. Even though they had supported the most famous punk band in the world at the most famous gig in the world, they walked away and carried on doing what they did.

DAVE HOWARD (keyboards – Solstice): It was punk, wasn't it? Things changed and things needed to change. We were used to bands like Zeppelin and Yes, who'd go off on long, meandering runs. Everything was pretty stale and it was wide open for someone to come along and rock the boat. We were run-of-the-mill. But if there were only fifty-odd people at that gig, how can it be so important? Even though we didn't like the Sex Pistols, a lot of good music came from them. It's nice, although we're under no illusions – we didn't influence anyone. It's nice to say to people, 'We played at that gig.' You can tell your grandchildren when you're in the old folks' home.

Neal Holden now works in the bar-coding industry. Dave Eyre is a cinema projectionist and is involved in local theatre. Dave 'Zok' Howard became an electronic engineer for Lancashire Police. He still plays and sings in pubs.

Audience member Alan Hempsall formed his own band in 1978 called Crispy Ambulance. After releasing a single on their own Aural Assault label, they signed to Tony Wilson's Factory Records. He now creates instrumental music aimed at film and video games and runs art events in south Manchester. To add to the increasingly convoluted connections to the Lesser Free Trade Hall, Hempsall once stood in for Joy Division frontman Ian Curtis after the epileptic singer suffered a particularly violent seizure.

ALAN HEMPSALL: About a month before he died he was a bit off-colour for a performance, so I got the call and stood in for him at this particular gig at Bury Town Hall. And a very eventful evening it was too. It had sold out fairly quickly – the momentum of Joy Division had well and truly built up. 'Love Will Tear Us Apart' was in the can and was about two months away from being released. I knew the stuff and they just said, 'Well, pick whatever you know the words to.' So it was great, just pick your favourite Joy Division songs and away we go. We then play 'Love Will Tear Us Apart' and 'Digital'. I then go off the stage, Ian Curtis then comes on and he felt well enough to do two very slow numbers. Then we all leave behind us a very confused audience. There was this loud crash and as we'd walked off some wag had just picked up an empty bottle and lobbed it at this enormous glass chandelier suspended over the stage, sending shards of glass showering down. Tony Wilson was by the door and I can just hear all these bottles breaking against the dressing-room door. Bernard [Sumner] is sat at the back of the dressing room with his feet up on the table and he was saying, 'I hate violence, it's just so temporary.' Meanwhile, Hooky is completely cut from different cloth – he has got two empty bottles and he's going, 'Come on! If there's enough of us here, we can take 'em!' Hooky's concerned because two of the roadies were out there and they're fighting to save the equipment. Hooky grabs me and shoves two empty beer bottles in my hand, drags me out on to the stage to be confronted with this row of people all just throwing empty pint-pots and bottles. Hooky, meanwhile, has now got Tony Wilson hanging on to him by his waist. Hooky's just dragging Tony round this stage shouting, 'Get back in! Get back in!'

Crispy Ambulance have reformed several times and still play live – sometimes on double-bills with fellow ex-Factory act Section 25. Hempsall – one of the most charming survivors of the Manchester music scene – is the only person I've found that swears he saw Tony Wilson there on that night on 4 June 1976.

ALAN HEMPSALL: It's just happenstance, for want of a better word. It would be fantastic to say, 'Oh, there was a magic that night.' I think you create your own magic. Yes, it's strange that I met Tony Wilson as a long-haired little gimp that night and later being on Tony's record label. I can't account for it but I'm not about to romanticise it either.

Stretford schoolboy Morrissey, along with guitarist and co-writer Johnny Marr, guided The Smiths through five years of swooning, literate tales of graveyard walks, back-alley fumblings and hopeless infatuations. They made a generation reach for the smelling salts. Piled high with expectation and weighed down by internal dissatisfaction and money wrangles, The Smiths collapsed in 1987, much to the indignation of their followers. Their albums stand the test of time better than any artists of the period and their influence can be traced via bands like The Sundays, Gene, Keane, Suede, Coldplay, The Killers and The Arctic

Monkeys. Johnny Marr, who copped for a lot of the public's blame at the time of the break-up, became a guitarist-for-hire and went on to work with another Free Trade Hall veteran, Bernard Sumner, in Electronic. He also turned out for Bryan Ferry, The The and The Pretenders. He's now a successful solo artist, with his 2014 album *Playland* receiving excellent reviews.

After a decade in the critical wilderness, Morrissey returned to favour in 2004 with the album *Irish Blood English Heart*. Always fond of 'penning an epistle', he released his wordy autobiography – called *Autobiography* – in 2013. His first novel – published in 2015 and called *List Of The Lost* – was described in the *Guardian* as 'An unpolished turd of a book, the stale excrement of Morrissey's imagination.' In 2006, on the subject of the Sex Pistols, whom he saw as a teenager, he told *NME*, 'I think they changed the world and I'm very grateful for that. I saw them three times at the very beginning and they were breathtaking and very necessary and I simply feel gratitude.'

Mark E. Smith, the young man who worked for the docks, formed The Fall a year after seeing the Sex Pistols. The job he created for himself in 1977 is the job he still holds today – lead singer of The Fall. It's possible that anyone who owns a musical instrument and lives in the Greater Manchester area has, at some point, been in The Fall. He's produced so many albums that compilers whiten at the task of annotating them. His acerbic reputation travels so far ahead of him that it arrives the day before your meeting is due to take place. When he was interviewed for this book, he drank Budweiser and could not have been more charming. He is a nice, somewhat frail man, who holds a unique place in British rock: that of a vague conscience. Having said that, much of his mystique could be attributed in no small part to the fact that it's very difficult to understand what he's actually saying.

MARK E. SMITH: We still feel very much outside the music business. The group's a lot younger than me now, which is a big improvement ... lot more spunk, you know? I'm trying to get more into that 'spoken word' thing. It's looking better than it has for a good five years now. Every time I leave a record company, they bring a bloody compilation out – you just get all these 'retros'. Which is why I'm a bit down on this kind of thing [talking about the past]. I don't look very far ahead, that's my problem. I don't look more than six months ahead. I would have a marvellous job in shipping if it weren't for the Sex Pistols. I'd probably have my own shipping company worldwide! Many times I've cursed the Sex Pistols!

Slaughter And The Dogs' guitarist Mick Rossi now lives in Los Angeles. As well as being a 'guitarist and full-time dreamer', he also, somewhat improbably, lists himself as an actor. Not so improbable after all, it appears. His debut film as a leading man was called *Played* and co-stars Val Kilmer, Gabriel Byrne, Vinnie Jones and Patsy Kensit. So there. It also featured a cameo from Pistols' guitarist Steve Jones. It's a thriller set in London and LA starring 'the little one out of Slaughter And The Dogs', as Peter Hook calls him, as an ex-con, called Ray Burns, out for revenge. Those keen on the art of the in-joke will know that Ray Burns is, of course, the given name of Captain Sensible of The Damned.

Rossi plays the part in his unusual Manamerican accent: 'Eight fookin' years and I didn't say a woird to nobody!' The film was not well reviewed.

Slaughter's singer, Wayne Barrett, now lives in France. He and Rossi still come together from time to time to play dates as Slaughter And The Dogs, especially at Blackpool's annual Rebellion festival. In 2015 they played Manchester's Ruby Lounge to mark their fortieth anniversary. They did the gig with most of their Lesser Free Trade Hall line-up, reuniting with drummer Brian Grantham and Howard Bates on bass.

HOWARD BATES: The opportunity came up because of the fortieth anniversary. There was a bit of ego on my part to think I'd love to do it again, just for the craic ... to get up there and have one more blast at it. Purely for the fun. So I thought, 'Why not?' It was odd seeing the guys in rehearsal because I hadn't seen Mick or Wayne for a long, long time.

MICK ROSSI: We rehearse in France. Wayne and I sit down and work on our show and what songs we're going to do. As soon as we strike up a chord or whatever, there's this little wry smile, yeah ... we've never lost that. There's always that tingle, you know? I remember we did one show in Blackpool at the Winter Gardens. I think it was the third song, called 'Boston Babies', which was on *Live At The Roxy*, and just hearing the entire crowd sing the lyrics, you kind of turn round and you go, 'Great, isn't it?' It's that little kid in you.

WAYNE BARRETT: I did a couple of mistakes, lyrics-wise, and there were these three guys at the Blackpool one and they were singing away. When I made a couple of mistakes on the lyrics they were going [tutting] like that and they're correcting me. I had to be really cautious of what I was singing after that, 'cause these three guys were censoring me. The three guys who were doing that, they were like nineteen or twenty. The vibes are still there, which is why I like working with Mr Rossi.

MICK ROSSI: Thank you, Mr Barrett.

WAYNE BARRETT: The confidence is total. I can turn away when I'm rehearsing and I know what Mike is doing and what he is going to be doing. He knows the same thing. We don't see each other for, let's say a year, but after around half an hour rehearsing, all that disappears.

MICK ROSSI: It's like a big family really. So it's a healthy vibe, no agendas, a lot of fun, no big shakes. Just fun and getting out there, and have a rocking good time.

Slaughter And The Dogs bass player Howard Bates now lives in Dorset and does 'a bit of this, bit of that, bit of the other.'

HOWARD BATES: Bit of property developing – not massive, just enough to keep to body and soul together. Maybe I'll get back into playing a bit, now I've dabbled. The juices have been flowing again since the reunion gig.

Eddie Garrity, otherwise known as Ed Banger, is still playing music, leading a glam-rock revival act and a revived version of The Nosebleeds.

EDDIE GARRITY: It does seem a long time ago now. The energy is still there when I play the songs and go out and do the odd gig now and again. At the time I never would have expected it to have lasted to this day, where there's still punk bands about. We all thought it would have been over in the first year or something. People were saying punk was dead but I don't think it ever will be – it'll just go on and on.

IAN MOSS: The immediate aftermath of the Sex Pistols was that there were bands that were worth making an effort to go and see. I found people who understood the way that I felt. I put a band together and had a thoroughly good time with that as well. The Hamsters was the first band. I had loads of bands: The Bears From Belle Vue Zoo, Mo Mo and The Dodos and numerous others. I spent too much time watching bands really. I worked in the fruit-and-veg trade, I ran my own shops too. I think punk was definitely life changing, I was at a party the other week and there I was, offering to fight two rugby players because they were making racist remarks. It's hard to let things go by. I went back to music a few years back. I'm with The Hamsters again and I run German Shepherd Records.

IAIN GREY (audience member): I'm actually in a band now, professionally: a cabaret band called The Steve Ferringo Band. I play all round Britain.

Not everyone at the Lesser Free Trade Hall joined a band. Audience member Vanessa Corley went on to run a vintage-clothing shop; Dawn Bradbury works in higher education; Peter Oldham became a professional photographer in south Manchester; Gary Ainsley became a hairdresser; Lorraine Joyce worked at Manchester Airport; John Berry is now semi-retired after working for United Utilities. Terry Mason – after touring the world with New Order – went into IT. *Penetration* editor Paul Welsh works for the NHS.

PAUL WELSH: All the people who have thought, 'I'd love to have been there on the night'... if they could go back in a time machine and have actually gone to the gig, I think they would have been disappointed. If you'd have been there on the night I don't think it would have been as exciting as it seemed. I think that, if Malcolm McLaren hadn't gotten the Sex Pistols together, some other band would have appeared doing the same sort of thing. It did change things – whether it was for the better or not I'm not sure. Some of the bands that came after were like kids banging on biscuit tins shouting about being unemployed – no talent whatsoever. People got the idea you could just go on stage and fool around. That's not what McLaren had in mind when he created the Sex Pistols.

STEVE SHY: I think the majority of people who grew out of punk didn't have an 'I don't give a fuck' attitude … But an 'I really, really care' attitude. That's why most of them have turned out the way they have. We became caring people.

Malcolm McLaren steered a course through life that included such ports of call as *The Great Rock 'n' Roll Swindle*, Ronnie Biggs, Bow Wow Wow, 'Buffalo Gals', scratching, skipping, opera/dance, waltz/dance, vougueing, films and running for Mayor of London. He died of cancer in 2010. He was buried in London's Highgate Cemetery to the sound of Sid Vicious's 'My Way'. His coffin featured the words 'Too Fast To Live, Too Young To Die'.

McLaren's former shop girl Pamela Rooke – aka Jordan – is still doing her own thing.

JORDAN: This is a bit off the wall really, but I'm a veterinary nurse and I breed Burmese cats and show them. I have some Grand Champion and Champion pussycats and I love my work. I've been very lucky; always wanted to work with Vivienne and Malcolm, I did. I wanted to work with Adam And The Ants and I did. I subsequently wanted to be a veterinary nurse and I did so. I've basically been asked to do each one – I haven't really had to do much for it, just been kind of lucky, I think. It's a funny thing, because Burmese cats are the punks of the feline world, no doubt about it. They're really very extrovert and they're very youthful – they stay young. If they could pogo, they would. I have always been very anti-nostalgia. I don't like people who constantly live in the past or try to recreate it, because I think it's frankly impossible. I don't think you can recreate it unless you're young. I think it's a young person's thing.

Chris Pye, producer of *So It Goes*, and the man who had to go for a little lie down after storming from the gallery to punch a Sex Pistol, became the vice president of Worldwide Formats for Sony Pictures Television International. He still works in television as a creative consultant.

CHRIS PYE: I'm a businessman. Making programmes is an exciting thing to do; it's a lot of fun. Being a business person, it's a different kind of fun. I think that making programmes like *So It Goes* and a few other shows I've made over the years makes you remember what fun it is to be a programme maker. You kind of miss it. Business meetings are not held on punk-rock lines. I think the legacy of punk is that you can do something that's completely outrageous and raw without really much musical content. I was the wrong generation to be sucked into it. I had a slight problem: I like harmony in music. Punk is not tremendously harmonious: there is not much three-part-harmony going on. I didn't object to the violence of it or the aggression of it, I just didn't like the sound of it. I never got into it or responded to it.

At the end of 2005 Peter Walker, the Director of *So It Goes*, retired from television directing at the age of seventy. He has mixed feelings about the Sex Pistols and the programme that he made with them in 1976.

PETER WALKER: I'm afraid punk, for me, never was an item; never became something I had a collection of at home. Looking back over the years and the things I've personally been involved with, there are three groups who immediately come to mind as being something that changed the way we look at music. I did the sound on The Doors, which was a programme that Granada made many, many years ago. I directed the Sex Pistols, which was like a shot in the arm and completely made us rethink. And I did a Wembley OB [outside broadcast] with Talking Heads for *The South Bank Show*. Those three groups immediately come to my mind – they made a hell of a lot of difference. It always amazed me later on, when I was working in London, I wandered into the Virgin Megastore on Oxford Street. I was looking up at the monitors where they had videos playing and that was my group [Sex Pistols] on the screen. I couldn't work out why. I thought this was really, really weird. Why are they playing my stuff? I felt I'd done more important things than that; more interesting things than that. Why have they got 'Anarchy In The UK' on? It's only because, from our perspective now, you can look back and say, well, yes, they were something special.

After years of standing empty and disused for years, the Free Trade Hall and the Lesser Free Trade Hall were reopened in 2004 as an upmarket hotel, The Radisson Blu Edwardian.

PHIL GRIFFIN (writer on architecture): For the second time in its life, the facade part of the Free Trade Hall has had something whacked onto the back of it, so having just about survived the Blitz to become essentially a 1950s concert hall, it survived the second Blitz of development and is now a five-star hotel. So a building that was named after a radical political movement, the Movement of Free Trade, is now the front of a globalised five-star hotel ... seems all right. It always had that kind of slight frisson of something ... from direct grant grammar-school speech days to trade-union meetings to strange, quirky, low-rent rock 'n' roll gigs. And now it's a five-star hotel.

While we're at it, whatever happened to everyone's favourite panty-friendly public house, Tommy Ducks? Sadly, Tommy Ducks is no longer there; it was demolished in the 1990s under bizarre and extremely swift circumstances.

PHIL GRIFFIN: It disappeared pretty bloody quickly, it has to be said ... over a weekend. Where Tommy Ducks was is now a Premier Lodge Hotel. Lots of people may mourn the loss but that's always the case, isn't it? So Tommy Ducks went and, along with it, the celebrated knickers on the ceiling ... which, actually, I think political correctness would have done away with in the fullness of time anyway.

Phil Singleton runs the revered sexpistols.net website from his home in Cheshire. Despite giving over most of his time to the band, he remains remarkably pragmatic when it comes to their place in pop culture.

PHIL SINGLETON: Some fans perceive the Pistols in a way that they can't possibly be in real life. There's a number of people that hold them in god-like esteem or think that they should behave in a certain way. People say it's all about anarchy. Well, it isn't actually about anarchy. You wouldn't be sat behind a computer screen if it was about anarchy. If you really believed in anarchy, you wouldn't be sat on the PC going on the message board, sending me emails. They seem to think that somehow the Sex Pistols are this force for anarchy and chaos. It's the real world and I wonder if that's why a lot of people get very agitated when the Pistols get back together – either they should be doing it but I'm not happy about the way they're doing it, or they're doing it in the way I think they should be doing it, but I can't get there. Emotions run very high.

In 1976 Paul Morley was a fanzine scribbler from Stockport. After a run on the *New Musical Express* and involvement with ZTT records (home of Frankie Goes To Hollywood) as a kind of hype ringmaster, he's now an author and cultural commentator. He co-authored *I'll Never Write My Memoirs* with Grace Jones. His book, *Nothing*, published in 2000, dealt with the suicide of his father and that of Joy Division's Ian Curtis. He has been working on a book about Tony Wilson for some years and has unerringly talked up *I Swear I Was There* at every opportunity over the years.

PAUL MORLEY: The thing about seeing the Pistols at the Lesser Free Trade Hall is that it's a curse. I know people of my age that weren't touched by punk – I can spot them a mile off. They're like middle-aged people were in the 1970s and the 1960s and the 1950s. Whereas someone touched by punk still kind of has a different kind of approach to life. One thing you could have said to any of us at that gig in '76 was that there was no way on earth that forty years later we would be nostalgic about it. We would have just hated you for suggesting it.

But, eventually, you get to that sort of pipe-smoking, brandy age when you realise it's important to point out how important it was and you're not necessarily being nostalgic. 1976 somehow feels closer now than it did in the Eighties. I think in the Eighties we were racing off, trying to sort of live up to our dreams and do things in a way we'd promised ourselves we would after seeing the Pistols. So it seemed a hundred years ago in the Eighties and now somehow it seems closer and easier to remember. I've got a funny, dreadful feeling that, when we do the fiftieth anniversary – as I suddenly realise we will be – it'll be, 'Oh, it was just like the other day'. There was a Manchester City football match in the 1960s: they got their lowest ever attendance when they played someone like Swindon – they got something like 6,000 at Maine Road. Three or four years later they won the Football League and 72,000 people claimed they were at that Swindon match. I've always had the same thing with the Lesser Free Trade Hall show. But now it seems absurd; how come there were only forty people there? It just seems daft because it was in *NME*, the Sex Pistols were *happening*. I guess those people that are embarrassed about the fact that their mums and dads wouldn't let them go and they were too scared of this strange thing that had come up from London – they're now trying to pretend that, in fact, they were there. But ... I swear I was there! For a long time you would say, 'If you don't believe me, fuck off'. Whereas now, I'm going to stand up and be counted.

Stage-invading art terrorist Jon the Postman moved to America, where he presumably changed his name to Jon the Mailman. After his return to the UK, he travelled the country trading records ... and worked for the Post Office.

JON THE POSTMAN: I'm trying to get out of the country. Because of what John Lydon said in 'God Save The Queen', 'No Future', it's come to pass and I'm off. Soon as possible ... this country is one big shit hole. Where? Germany, hopefully. I've been to California before, lived in

France. I want to try something different. I believe you can get a cheap pint there and people behave themselves and I am looking forward to it ... touch wood.

Jon The Postman died in July 2015. His passing was covered by everyone from the *Guardian* to Hollywood.com.

STEVE SHY: Sadly, I reached my sixtieth and he didn't. It's a big shame. His mind was amazing. He could always tell you the last time he saw you, what gig it was, who the support band was and what we were drinking. I believe it took £200-worth of cardboard boxes to put his records in after he'd gone. They played Joy Division at the funeral. And some of Jon's own stuff. He'd put a free bar on for us. Thanks, Jon. They gave us a playlist of songs that were going to be played during the do afterwards. It was all MC5, *Nuggets* stuff, 1960s garage, The Fall. It was memorable.

DAWN BRADBURY: Very sad. I was at his funeral. They handed out lyric sheets to 'Louie Louie'. There was an event a few months later to celebrate his life. Jon The Postman was still holding court, even though he wasn't there. A few notable absences, some of the more famous punks. I suppose some of the bands have got other commitments. Would have been nice to see to see some of them knocking about. It was a great night, celebrating Jon's bizarre eclectic musical life. Then we had his posthumous sixtieth birthday party. He wanted it in Berlin. It went ahead without him. A great weekend in Berlin for ageing punk rockers!

Sex Pistols

| Malcolm McLaren | 4.6.76 | £212.50 | 50p. |
| Lesser Hall | Takings £14 | | |

| Howard Stafford | 20.7.76 | £425 | £1 |
| Lesser Hall | Takings £121 | | |

Manchester council records showing final takings for both gigs. Thousands may claim to have attended but, with £14 takings on 50p tickets, we have our proof that a mere twenty eight lucky people paid to see that first iconic concert.

© *Manchester Libraries Information and Archive*

CHAPTER TEN

PRAXIS MAKES PERFECT

The Mancunian memories of those involved in the events of 1976 are, as I think you've realised by now, a touch varied. Some people who swear they were there are unshakable in the belief that their version of events is the right one, only to be directly contradicted by the person who was standing next to them. Trying to get a definitive version of events is like looking at the past through a fractured telescope ... that's just had ten pints of bitter poured into it. It's not easy to get to the truth. Some people, though, can definitely prove they were there. Because they kept their ticket.

JOHN BERRY: I must have been aware at the time that the ticket was worth hanging onto. I was a bit of a hoarder but I don't think I have any other ticket stubs from that era, apart from that one. It's in a frame in the toilet. Most people don't see it when they go for a slash. It's such an innocuous thing. It's just a rag of paper.

It's often assumed that Mick Hucknall, lead singer of Simply Red, was at the Lesser Free Trade Hall on 4 June 1976 – it's in *24 Hour Party People* so it must be true. In 2003 Hucknall was asked about his memories of the event in *Q* magazine. His reply couldn't be clearer: 'I didn't see the Pistols in 1976. It's a myth. I could put my hand up and lie, but I didn't go. People claim they've got it on film, but unless I was asleep and sleepwalked in I wasn't there ... I'd love to have gone.'

In 2010 Hucknall made a Simply Red special for ITV called *For The Last Time*. As part of the show, Hucknall took presenter Christine Bleakley on a tour of Manchester, including a chat outside the Free Trade Hall ... to talk about seeing the Sex Pistols. 'This was the first time I saw something that was my generation,' he told Bleakley. 'They were kind of spotty and kind of messy, like we were. The Free Trade Hall was one of the main music venues when I was fifteen or sixteen. We started rehearsing [with The Frantic Elevators] after we'd seen the Sex Pistols.'

I think you get the point. No wonder the story of the Sex Pistols at the Lesser Free Trade Hall has become a little knotted over the years. A mixture of desire, memory-lapse, self reinvention and selective access to the media has made things get very confused indeed. One of Tony Wilson's favourite words – and he had many – was 'praxis'. 'Doing something and then, only afterwards, finding out why you did it,' as he once described it.

JOHN MAHER: This is the sort of analysis that only happens after the event, when people start to mythologise ... If it hadn't been for those two gigs, this wouldn't have happened and that wouldn't have happened. You can't prove or disprove that, can you? How much of what I'm saying right now is influenced by what I've heard or read? There was obviously something in the air – things had to change. If Howard hadn't gone to see the Pistols and brought them up to Manchester, something else would have happened. The conditions were right. I think there's an awful lot of that gone on over the years. You see all these documentaries about the punk years. How many times have we seen that footage of rubbish piled up in the streets? About how Manchester was a desolate place? When I was growing up as a kid, I wasn't thinking, 'God, this is a really desolate place'. I read Morrissey's biography recently. He was brought up a few streets away from me. At the start of the book he's describing what it was like round our way. I *do not* recognise his version of it. He's got a florid imagination and it doesn't fit with my reality, but then, if that's how he remembers it, it's up to him to describe it like that. We all see it through different eyes ... and I certainly don't see it through Morrissey's eyes.

History is largely written by those with access to typewriters – and sometimes these people can make things worse. The desire for the truth to lie a certain way after the fact can get the better of us, no matter how high-minded we purport our intentions to be. This is the third edition of this book – fourth if you count an Italian version produced in 2011. In every edition so far, Mark E. Smith of The Fall has been put in the 'gig one' section. The reality is that, on the day I interviewed him and I started my first question about the events at the Lesser Free Trade with the Sex Pistols in 1976, he replied, 'Oh yeah ... Buzzcocks, Slaughter And The Dogs and all that.' He was at the second gig but it appears I really, *really* wanted him to be 'gig one'. So, consciously or unconsciously, I tweaked it. It's only now, going back over the interviews, that I realised what I'd done. I'd changed it to suit my own purposes. Nothing to do with Smith. Purely my own doing. No wonder it's so difficult to unravel a story like the Sex Pistols and the Lesser Free Trade Hall.

For me, though, the Sex Pistols are, in a way, the least interesting part of the story. The myth, the mistakes and the mangling of the truth has always been where it's at; in true punk fashion, it's about the audience, not the band. But it has always left me with an itch: *all these years obsessing about a single gig by the Sex Pistols and I've never actually seen the Sex Pistols.*

On 27 June 2002 I put that right. Here I was, walking across a sports field in London with my twelve-year-old son Jake. In a pleasant nod to the summer of 1976, it's achingly hot. So much so that I sign up for a credit card from a promotions stand so I can get a free hat for Jake to keep the sun off him. Credit-card promotion stands at punk gigs? Things really have changed.

We gingerly pick our way through a becalmed sea of zonked-out punks who have taken the decision to shell out £26 to see a gig at Crystal Palace and then get comatose-pissed on cider before it even starts.

For this is the Pistol's Jubilee – Pistols At The Palace. There's unpleasantness to get through before the main act. Namely the falling-down hopeless Libertines and American shouty-types And You Will Know Us By The Trail of Dead. The main act is the Sex Pistols and I am here for two reasons. One: to satisfy my curiosity, and two to allow my son the pleasure of saying, *I Swear I Was There*.

PHIL SINGLETON: The bottom line is, it's all about entertainment. When it all boils down, there isn't that much difference between the Sex Pistols, The Rolling Stones, The Beatles and, dare I say it, The Osmonds. I think people have to be quite honest when they look back and say punk rock was entertainment. I could turn round now and say, 'Green Day aren't punk, that's not what it's about.' They think they're punk, the people who go along say they're punk, what right has anyone to say it's not punk? Lydon reckons that Crystal Palace was one of the best Pistols gigs ever. Twenty thousand hooligans in a field and no trouble. Mind you, most people there were too old to cause trouble.

As the harsh sun begins to set over the burger vans and beer tents, a sea of hefty punks begin pushing forward, bellowing, 'Reason, reason, reason.' Then the band are led on by Lydon, sporting a black shirt bearing the word 'Sorry'. 'We are the Sex Pistols,' he announces. 'A bunch of two-bob cunts.' Oh, Lordy. Best keep mum about that bit when we get home.

The first number is a cover version. Not 'Steppin' Stone' or 'No Fun' but Hawkwind's hippy, space-rock anthem 'Silver Machine'. Brilliant. The Solstice boys would have loved it. My son is slightly bemused – this was not what he was expecting. There's even a bubble machine. The Pistols bang through their slim repertoire and tell us that they love us. After the gig has finished, we manage to miss every bus imaginable but we're happy walking to where we hope there's a taxi rank in the warm night breeze. We're lost but we've seen the Sex Pistols. You don't get father-and-son moments like this at Centre Parcs. We stay the night at a hotel built on the site of the former Croydon airport. The next morning we eat our full English in the restaurant. On the tables dotted around us are gentlemen of a certain age, munching on eggs, bacon and toast. We pack up and leave for home.

Rather fantastically, my son will, from that day forward, claim that the first gig he ever went to was 'Pistols at the Palace'. He and I both know it was actually Irish popstrels B*Witched some three years earlier. But saying that the first gig you ever saw was the Sex Pistols just sounds better. I get it.

See? It's a very common problem.

CAST OF CHARACTERS

GARY AINSLEY – AUDIENCE MEMBER.

WAYNE BARRETT – LEAD SINGER, SLAUGHTER AND THE DOGS.

HOWARD BATES – BASS PLAYER, SLAUGHTER AND THE DOGS.

JOHN BERRY – AUDIENCE MEMBER.

WILL BIRCH – FORMER DRUMMER WITH THE KURSAAL FLYERS, AUTHOR OF *NO SLEEP TILL CANVEY ISLAND – THE GREAT PUB ROCK REVOLUTION*.

DAWN BRADBURY – AUDIENCE MEMBER.

STEVE 'SHY' BURKE – AUDIENCE MEMBER.

GORDON BURNS – TV PRESENTER.

VANESSA CORLEY – AUDIENCE MEMBER.

HOWARD DEVOTO – LEAD SINGER OF BUZZCOCKS AND MAGAZINE.

STEVE DIGGLE – AUDIENCE MEMBER, BUZZCOCKS BASS PLAYER AND, LATER, GUITARIST.

DAVE EYRE – SOUNDMAN, SOLSTICE.

EDDIE GARRITY – AUDIENCE MEMBER AND LEAD SINGER OF ED BANGER AND THE NOSEBLEEDS.

IAIN GREY – AUDIENCE MEMBER.

PHIL GRIFFIN – ARCHITECTURAL WRITER.

ALAN HEMPSALL – AUDIENCE MEMBER AND LEAD SINGER OF CRISPY AMBULANCE.

NEAL HOLDEN – LIGHTING ENGINEER, SOLSTICE.

PETER HOOK – BASS PLAYER WITH JOY DIVISION/NEW ORDER/MONACO

DAVE 'ZOK' HOWARD – KEYBOARD PLAYER, SOLSTICE.

JORDAN – SHOP ASSISTANT AND PUNK MUSE. PUNK ROCK MADE HUMAN.

LORRAINE JOYCE – AUDIENCE MEMBER.

HOWARD KINGSTON – LEAD SINGER, GENTLEMEN.

JOHN MAHER – BUZZCOCKS DRUMMER.

TERRY MASON – AUDIENCE MEMBER.

GLEN MATLOCK – BASS PLAYER WITH THE SEX PISTOLS.

MALCOLM MCLAREN – MANAGER OF THE SEX PISTOLS.

CAST OF CHARACTERS

IAN MOSS – AUDIENCE MEMBER.

PAUL MORLEY – AUDIENCE MEMBER AND *NEW MUSICAL EXPRESS* JOURNALIST.

PETER OLDHAM – AUDIENCE MEMBER AND PHOTOGRAPHER.

JON THE POSTMAN – AUDIENCE MEMBER WITH SELF-EXPLANATORY DAY JOB.

CHRIS PYE – PRODUCER OF *SO IT GOES* TV SHOW.

MICK ROSSI – GUITAR PLAYER WITH SLAUGHTER AND THE DOGS.

PETE SHELLEY – GUITAR PLAYER AND LATER LEAD VOCALIST WITH BUZZCOCKS.

PHIL SINGLETON – SEX-PISTOLS.NET.

MARK E. SMITH – LEAD SINGER OF THE FALL.

BERNARD SUMNER – AUDIENCE MEMBER, JOY DIVISION/NEW ORDER/ELECTRONIC

PETER WALKER – DIRECTOR OF *SO IT GOES* TV SHOW.

PAUL WELSH – AUDIENCE MEMBER AND EDITOR OF *PENETRATION* MAGAZINE.

TONY WILSON – TV PRESENTER AND FORMER HEAD OF FACTORY RECORDS.

DICK WITTS – AUDIENCE MEMBER AND TV PRESENTER.